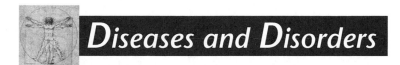

Diseases and Disorders

Fetal Alcohol Syndrome

Diseases and Disorders

Fetal Alcohol Syndrome

Titles in the Diseases and Disorders series include:

Diseases and Disorders

Fetal Alcohol Syndrome

by Gail B. Stewart

LUCENT BOOKS
An imprint of Thomson Gale, a part of The Thomson Corporation

THOMSON

™

GALE

Detroit • New York • San Francisco • San Diego • New Haven, Conn.
Waterville, Maine • London • Munich

LIBRARY OF CONGRESS CATALOGING-IN-PUBLICATION DATA

Stewart, Gail, 1949–
  Fetal alcohol syndrome / by Gail Stewart.
    p. cm. — (Diseases and disorders)
Summary: Discusses the causes and symptoms of fetal alcohol syndrome and what is being done to raise awareness of the disease.
  Includes bibliographical references and index.
  ISBN 1-59018-591-9 (hard cover : alk. paper)
  1. Fetal alcohol syndrome—Juvenile literature. I. Title. II. Series: Diseases and disorders series
  RG629.F45S74 2004
  618.3'26861—dc22
                                                    2004015186

Printed in the United States of America

Table of Contents

"The Most Difficult Puzzles Ever Devised"

CHARLES BEST, ONE of the pioneers in the search for a cure for diabetes, once explained what it is about medical research that intrigued him so. "It's not just the gratification of knowing one is helping people," he confided, "although that probably is a more heroic and selfless motivation. Those feelings may enter in, but truly, what I find best is the feeling of going toe to toe with nature, of trying to solve the most difficult puzzles ever devised. The answers are there somewhere, those keys that will solve the puzzle and make the patient well. But how will those keys be found?"

Since the dawn of civilization, nothing has so puzzled people—and often frightened them, as well—as the onset of illness in a body or mind that had seemed healthy before. A seizure, the inability of a heart to pump, the sudden deterioration of muscle tone in a small child—being unable to reverse such conditions or even to understand why they occur was unspeakably frustrating to healers. Even before there were names for such conditions, even before they were understood at all, each was a reminder of how complex the human body was, and how vulnerable.

While our grappling with understanding diseases has been frustrating at times, it has also provided some of humankind's most heroic accomplishments. Alexander Fleming's accidental discovery in 1928 of a mold that could be turned into penicillin has resulted in the saving of untold millions of lives. The isolation of the enzyme insulin has reversed what was once a death sentence for anyone with diabetes. There have been great strides in combating conditions for which there is not yet a cure, too. Medicines can help AIDS patients live longer, diagnostic tools such as mammography and ultrasounds can help doctors find tumors while they are treatable, and laser surgery techniques have made the most intricate, minute operations routine.

This "toe-to-toe" competition with diseases and disorders is even more remarkable when seen in a historical continuum. An astonishing amount of progress has been made in a very short time. Just 200 years ago, the existence of germs as a cause of some diseases was unknown. In fact, it was less than 150 years ago that a British surgeon named Joseph Lister had difficulty persuading his fellow doctors that washing their hands before delivering a baby might increase the chances of a healthy delivery (especially if they had just attended to a diseased patient)!

Each book in Lucent's Diseases and Disorders series explores a disease or disorder and the knowledge that has been accumulated (or discarded) by doctors through the years. Each book also examines the tools used for pinpointing a diagnosis, as well as the various means that are used to treat or cure a disease. Finally, new ideas are presented—techniques or medicines that may be on the horizon.

Frustration and disappointment are still part of medicine, for not every disease or condition can be cured or prevented. But the limitations of knowledge are being pushed outward constantly; the "most difficult puzzles ever devised" are finding challengers every day.

"Where Do I Start?"

D ENISE AND HER husband, Tom, live in a suburb of St. Paul, Minnesota. They adopted their son Benny when he was just eight months old. Denise says that they were delighted when their adoption caseworker called and said she had a little boy for them. "We were *so* happy," she says. "We had tried for several years—unsuccessfully—to conceive, and it seemed that adoption was the best way for us to go. When we got the call, we were overjoyed."

"He Never Reacted"

Denise says that because they were first-time parents, they were unaware that anything was wrong with Benny at first. "He was really small," she says. "I did realize that—only because my neighbor had a little girl who was four months old, half as old as Benny, but she was bigger than he was. But as the weeks and months went by, we realized there were things about Benny that were more odd than just his being small for his age."

Benny did not smile or interact with his parents. He did not seem to enjoy being held or talked to. "He'd get stiff, as though he was afraid," Denise remembers. "He never reacted when I sang to him. I thought babies all liked that, but Benny just looked startled, you know? At first Tom kidded me that it was just because my voice was off-key or something—I do have a bad sense of pitch, I know. But weeks were going by, and Benny really seemed to prefer lying in his crib to being touched or handled."

Their pediatrician did not think there was anything physically wrong with the baby, and suggested that Benny might be allergic to milk. "We changed to soy, we fed him at different times, we did everything we could, but nothing changed," Denise says. "It wasn't an allergy, it wasn't anything like that. We didn't find out what was wrong with our son until he was five."

"Where Do I Start?"

It was then that Benny was diagnosed with a disease known as fetal alcohol syndrome, or FAS. "It was because his mother drank quite heavily when she was pregnant with him," says Denise. "As a result of the alcohol that went into his system, his brain didn't develop right."

Pregnant mothers who consume alcohol run the risk of giving birth to children with fetal alcohol syndrome like this boy.

Asked what kind of problems that means for Benny, Denise sighs. "Where do I start?" she says. "He has a lot of trouble talking. He gets confused if I ask him to repeat a sentence. He won't be able to do it without a lot of help. He gets frustrated very easily, and that usually means tantrums. Benny's six now, but emotionally he's more like a three-year-old. He doesn't interact very well with other people, especially other children. He still wears a diaper at night.

"Both Tom and I love Benny with all our hearts," Denise adds. "I wouldn't love him more if he didn't have FAS. I'd worry a lot less, though. The disabilities he has will be with him his whole life, because fetal alcohol syndrome is not curable. There is no medicine or therapy that can help him do addition problems or read a story, or many of the things that other kids do. He may eventually learn some of these things, but he won't learn them quickly. That's just the way things will be."[1]

Chapter 1

A Devastating Disease

THOUSANDS OF BABIES are born each year in the United States with birth defects caused by alcohol consumption. About forty thousand children annually are diagnosed with the disease, but researchers say that as many as 95 percent of those with FAS go undiagnosed. They believe that the number of babies born with the disease is far higher.

Even with the relatively low estimate of babies affected by the disease each year, FAS accounts for more birth defects than all other causes combined, including Down syndrome, muscular dystrophy, and spina bifida. And though not everyone born with FAS is mentally retarded, the disease is still the leading cause of mental retardation in the United States.

"Foolish, Drunken and Hare-Brained Women"

It was not until the late 1960s that fetal alcohol syndrome was investigated for the first time. Until then, even though some throughout history had raised the idea that alcohol might be unhealthy to unborn children, there was no scientific data that supported their suspicions. As long ago as 330 B.C., the Greek philosopher Aristotle noted, "Foolish, drunken and hare-brained women most often bring forth children like unto themselves, morose and languid."[2] In ancient Sparta and Carthage, there was a custom prohibiting newlyweds from drinking on their wedding night in order to prevent conceiving a "damaged" child.

In 1726 British physicians speculated that alcohol was poisonous to the unborn, and as a result, too many youngsters were destined to become a drain on society. In a special report to Parliament, the College of Physicians wrote, "Parental drinking is a cause of weak, feeble, and distempered children, who must be, instead of an advantage and strength, a charge to their country."[3]

About Face

As time went on, it seemed that medical science was more and more certain that alcohol was indeed harmful to unborn children.

A poster from the 1920s urging Americans to support Prohibition suggests that women and children are the principal victims of alcohol abuse.

The Shadow of Danger

U.S.
FINE MELLOW
WHISKEY

If you believe that the traffic in Alcohol does more harm than good- *help stop it!*

This certainty continued through Prohibition, a period in the United States (from 1920 to 1933) when laws made it illegal for people to drink, sell, or make alcoholic beverages.

When Prohibition ended, however, and the laws banning liquor were repealed, many of the earlier beliefs about the evils of alcohol were questioned. Some people scoffed at the notion that alcohol caused problems in unborn children, believing that the idea was simply propaganda circulated by proponents of Prohibition in order to ban liquor in the United States. By the mid-1930s, some doctors were even reassuring their pregnant patients that there was no harm in a drink or two daily for pregnant women, as a means of relaxing.

"It Can Now Be Stated Categorically"

Some scientists questioned earlier research that indicated that women who drank while pregnant were more likely to suffer stillbirths or miscarriages or have sickly children. They proposed that those problems were caused not by alcohol but by the poverty, bad hygiene, and poor eating habits of the mothers who drank. Even if alcohol were to blame for the death of or disease in the unborn, some social scientists reasoned that it could be looked on as a boon. They insisted that since most of the drinking women were "lower class" or "undesirable," the alcohol was acting as a selective poison, weeding out the weaker, less desirable members of society.

By the 1950s, alcohol use among pregnant women was on the rise. And few worried about the effects on the unborn. In his 1964 book *Life Before Birth,* Dr. Ashley Montague argued that there was absolutely nothing to worry about, no matter how much a pregnant woman were to drink:

> Unexpectedly, alcohol in the form of beverages, even in immoderate amounts, has no apparent effect on a child before birth. . . . It can now be stated categorically . . . that no matter how great the amounts of alcohol taken by the mother—or the father, for that matter—neither the germ cells nor the development of the child will be affected. . . . An amount of alcohol in the blood that would kill the mother is not enough even to irritate the tissues of the child. [4]

A Disease Discovered and Named

Four years after Montague's book was published, a group of French scientists had far different news to report. They had been tracking 127 children born to alcoholic mothers and found a series of effects that they blamed on alcohol exposure while the children were in the fetal stage. The scientists identified stunted growth patterns, deformities of the face, and defects of the nervous system. They also documented a series of behavioral and emotional problems suffered by the children. The French study received only modest attention, however, because it was published in a small French journal and was never translated into English.

In 1973 another article dealing with the effects of alcohol on unborn children appeared in the prestigious British medical journal *Lancet*. The article documented the work of a group of scientists headed by Dr. David Smith and Dr. Kenneth Jones from the University of Washington. They studied infants born to alcoholic mothers at Harborview Hospital in Seattle.

Besides noting the range of physical deformities of the infants, Smith and Jones described the babies' failure to gain weight, their apparent disinterest in nursing, their poor suckling ability, and how infrequently they cried for attention. The doctors sought the assistance of a child psychologist, who found that the infants had varying degrees of brain damage as well. Finally, Smith and Jones gave this collection of symptoms its name: fetal alcohol syndrome.

The article by Smith and Jones received a great deal of international attention. Research groups were formed in a number of countries to study alcohol and its effects on their populations. Scientists wanted to know if fetal alcohol syndrome was found more often in certain groups within a population. They were interested, too, in long-range effects of the disease. Were there cures or therapies that could help a child born with FAS? The questions about this new disease seemed endless.

Fetal Alcohol Effects

As more and more research supported the findings of the University of Washington team, scientists compiled the characteristics

Butterflies

In this excerpt from her book Fetal Alcohol Syndrome: A Guide for Families and Communities, *Ann Streissguth, one of the pioneers of FAS research, describes her first encounter with several young children who had been damaged by prenatal drinking.*

It was January 1973. I was in shock. I had just finished administering a psychological examination to the seventh young child in the troup that Jones and Smith, my dysmorphology colleagues [physicians with expertise in congenital malformations], had asked me to see. Although the seven children represented three racial groups and were not themselves related, they looked eerily alike: small, sparkly eyes; small heads; and an appearance about the mouth that appeared as though they were pursing their lips even when they weren't smiling. Except for the two who were still infants and the one who was so flaccid she was carried in the arms of her mother, the other children had a wispy, flighty quality. I thought to myself that these children who were so curiously and surprisingly unafraid of me were like butterflies.

These children clearly had brain damage. . . . Each of these children had experienced damage to his or her central nervous system that was apparent in his or her erratic movements, poor coordination, flighty attentional states, and poor performance on psychological tests, despite a captivatingly alert and bright-eyed manner.

"You think that alcohol causes this?" I asked incredulously of Jones and Smith.

into a profile of a child with FAS. Initially, doctors believed that a child could be considered to be suffering the effects of FAS if three particular criteria were met.

The first sign was a slow pattern of growth in the child. Second were abnormalities of the central nervous system. Such abnormalities could be mental retardation or a very small head size. An unusually small head can indicate a problem with brain development, a condition known as microcephaly. Finally, a child with FAS exhibited facial deformities, such as a very thin upper lip, a flattened face, or smaller than normal eye openings.

As more research was done, however, scientists realized that many children whose mothers had a history of drinking while pregnant had only some of the signs of FAS. For example, they displayed a reduced ability to learn and a slow growth rate yet lacked the physical deformities identified with FAS. Scientists used the term *fetal alcohol effects* (FAE) to describe these children.

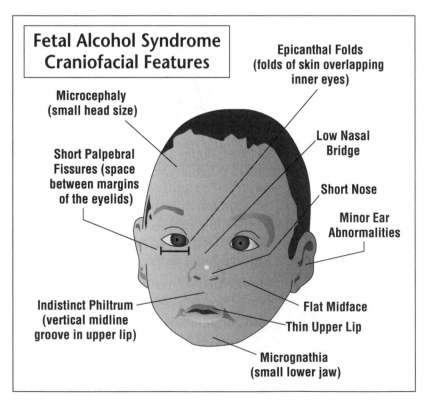

FAS and FAE

At first, researchers thought that FAE was a milder form of the disease. After all, FAE children were less likely to be mentally retarded and did not exhibit the physical abnormalities that many children with FAS do. However, over the last decade, researchers have altered this view. They now say that although children with FAE have been spared the physical deformities, their brains are still damaged. They may or may not be mentally retarded, but they also may have more serious behavioral and emotional problems, most of which, unlike physical problems associated with FAS, go undiagnosed for years.

"We never knew David had birth defects from alcohol," says his mother, Darla. "I've seen pictures of babies and little kids with fetal alcohol syndrome, you know, and he doesn't look like them. He isn't retarded, either. But he's always had *a lot* of school problems—and a lot of social problems, too. We wouldn't have known about the FAE without Davy's birth father coming forward. We knew Davy's birth mother had been in trouble with the law, but we didn't know she was an alcoholic until [the father] wrote us a letter, through the adoption agency. That really opened our eyes, and it answered a lot of questions, too."[5]

Because FAE is no longer thought of as a less severe form of fetal alcohol syndrome, many experts have pushed for eliminating the term *FAE* altogether. They argue that FAS should be thought of as an umbrella disease that can show itself in a number of different ways.

"It's Just Beer, Right?"

Not all women who drink while they are pregnant deliver a baby with FAS. Twyla, a thirty-year-old mother of four, says that her youngest, Arthur, is the only one of her children who has been affected by her drinking. "I don't consider myself an alcoholic," she says. "And I probably drank more with my older two than with Arthur and his sister. That's why I was surprised when Arthur was diagnosed [with FAS]."[6]

Scientists are not yet sure why some pregnant women who drink deliver healthy, normal babies, while others deliver babies with

FAS. They do know that about 50 percent of pregnant alcoholics will have babies with FAS. As dangerous as the woman who drinks every day during her pregnancy is the binge-drinker, someone who consumes five or more drinks at one sitting, such as at a celebration or party. However, it is not only heavy drinkers who are putting their unborn children at risk. There are risks for moderate or occasional drinkers, too.

It is also clear that it makes no difference what sort of alcoholic beverage a pregnant woman drinks, for they can all be dangerous—beer, wine, and even wine coolers. Twyla says that she believed she was being careful during her pregnancy by limiting her drinking to beer. "I had no idea," she says. "I was staying away from hard stuff. I thought a couple of beers after my shift [at a nearby factory] wouldn't hurt. It's just beer, right? But it was me drinking beer that hurt Arthur. I know that. But you can see why I wonder why my other three haven't got the same thing he does. It just doesn't make sense."[7]

Scientists are still trying to determine why the disease occurs in some cases and not others. But for a pregnant woman who drinks, pediatric specialist Sterling Clarren compares her chances of producing a healthy child to a drunk driver's chances on the highway. "If you get really, really drunk at a restaurant and then drive home, will you have an accident? Not necessarily. You might get home okay," he says. "Are you at a high risk for having an accident? Yes—a very high risk."[8]

Groups at Risk

Although FAS can victimize any fetus, regardless of its race, ethnicity, or economic class, it is not surprising that the disease is more prevalent in groups in which alcohol abuse is a big problem. In the United States, FAS is statistically more common among babies born to poor or uneducated women. Teenage mothers tend to be more apt to drink while pregnant, too.

In the United States as a whole, approximately three babies are diagnosed with FAS out of every one thousand births. However, experts warn that that figure is low, since so many victims of FAS are not diagnosed until they are older. There are segments of the

A pregnant woman reaches for a glass of hard liquor. Pregnant women who consume any type of alcohol, even in moderation, can give birth to children with FAS.

"My Life Wasn't the Best"

Though many women do not admit to using alcohol during pregnancy, reporter Jane Kwiatkowski interviewed a mother who was willing to discuss her alcoholism, as well as the child who died from the effects of prenatal alcohol exposure. The following excerpt is from an article in the Buffalo News *titled "Damage Done."*

[Cynthia Cray explains,] "I started drinking when I was in high school, but it wasn't habit-forming until 1981, when I had my daughter. Then I really started to drink. I liked the high, the way it took me away. My life wasn't the best. I got the taste of gin and grapefruit juice and I went crazy."

Cray lives on Moslem Street with her 8-year-old son, Christopher. Another child lives with her father. Her grown daughter, Tiffany, lives on her own. Baby Robin was buried two years ago.

"I used with my other children and they came out healthy, so being ignorant I continued to drink. . . . I drank every day—three or four 40s of Magnum or Molson Ice. I did it to block out a lot of things, but in reality you drink because you want to drink." . . .

Robin was born with heart disease, kidney disease, liver failure and an undersized brain. But Cray wanted to provide a home for her daughter, so she learned to care for her.

"She was learning how to stand. She was smiling. She brought me joy and my self-worth. She hung in there," Cray said. "She had more courage than I ever did. It was a battle and she was fighting, but her lungs were giving out and she could not breathe."

population where FAS is much higher. In certain Native American communities, for example, more than half of the children show symptoms of FAS.

Ida, an Oglala Sioux Indian, insists that that should not be a surprise. "The worst is Pine Ridge Reservation, in South Dakota," she says. "I'll tell you, it's the poorest place in the United States. A year ago, in 2003, they estimated 65 percent of the children on the reservation have symptoms [of FAS]. There's generations of alcoholics living there, no jobs, no future. They've lost their way—that's the best way to say it. They got kids there—twelve, thirteen years old—drinking on a regular basis, every day, you know? They sit out on the curb, in plain view of all the people, and they drink."

Ida claims that many of the teens with drinking problems are getting pregnant. "They're having babies, these young girls," she says. "These mothers, and these little babies they're bringing in to the world, they got no chance. It's all they see, it's all they know. They've lost their way. And that's a tragedy for the Indian people. We're losing so many of our own, and so many unborn."[9]

A group of Native Americans on a Nebraska reservation drink beer. In some Native American communities, more than half of the children have FAS.

"Who Wouldn't Want to Drink?"

The United States is not the only country with an FAS problem. There are a number of nations, such as Russia, Canada, and Chile, working to address their own growing incidence of the disease. However, it is South Africa that has the highest national rate of any country in the world; it was estimated in 2002 that in the southern part of the country, one child out of every ten has fetal alcohol syndrome.

The root of the problem there is the long-standing practice by white farmers and vineyard owners of paying their workers with a flask of wine instead of money. This practice, known as the "tot" system, was outlawed in 1961, when it became apparent that alcoholism had become an epidemic among the workers and their families. Even so, the tot system continues in large areas of South Africa, where wine is cheap, and it is not uncommon to see six- and seven-year-olds drinking openly.

Many South Africans are aware of the problem, and say it is made worse because of the abject poverty of the workers, as well as their lack of hope that things will improve in the future. Magdelena Booysen, who gave birth to a son with severe FAS three years ago, says she was warned by her doctor that she might be endangering her unborn child. However, she admits that drinking was the only thing that could make her forget her depression. "In these conditions," she says, pointing to her home's broken windows and leaky roof, "who wouldn't want to drink?" [10]

Human Costs

In South Africa, the United States, and other nations where the number of FAS victims is growing yearly, health officials stress that the costs of the disease—both human and financial—are severe. "First and foremost, it's the children themselves," says Mary, who adopted a baby with FAS two years ago. "They will struggle all their lives with disabilities. Some of them don't have the same life expectancy as other children—their hearts have valve problems, their kidneys may not work right. The ones who don't have the physical birth defects have lifelong problems of other kinds. Everything is a struggle." [11]

Ireland's FAS Problem

In the following excerpt from an article for the Belfast News Letter *called "Drinking Mothers Damage Unborn Babies," the reporter argues that Ireland is not taking its fetal alcohol syndrome problem seriously, compared to doctors in the United States.*

Every year in Ulster, some 25 babies will be born severely damaged because their mothers drank throughout their pregnancies. Many of these mothers will be single parents, some will have wayward partners, but some will have long term partners. In America they would be advised not to drink at all during pregnancy. Yet here in Northern Ireland government sources still give them "drinking guidelines" despite the growing evidence of the damage alcohol causes to the fetus. . . .

[FAS advocate] Anne Townsend . . . says women have to be alerted to the facts. "America is well tuned into the problems, so we have to make sure women here are told the truth. We have issued a leaflet which sets out the government guidelines on drinking but ideally every woman should plan to stop drinking alcohol before conceiving. No one knows how much drinking harms a baby, but it is known that it directly affects the developing baby as do other substances such as nicotine and other drugs. Women have to remember that every time they drink a glass of wine their baby is drinking two. Even after the baby is born, alcohol can be passed to the baby in small amounts through breast milk."

One adoptive father agrees. He and his wife adopted their daughter eight years ago, when she was a year old. "Her birth defects are less physical and more to do with her learning and her behavior," he says. "She's got some vision problems, but that will be corrected over time. But she's most likely never going to be able to live on her own completely. Her IQ is below normal, and she has trouble telling time. Her mom and I understand that she'll always need outside help, just to get along."[12]

Fetal alcohol syndrome takes a toll on the families of victims, too. "The kids [with FAS] have so many extra needs different from normal kids," says Anne, whose adopted seventeen-year-old son has FAS. "This isn't a complaint, it's just a reality. We work hard just teaching our kids things other parents don't spend much thought on.

"Our son will be eighteen in two months, but in so many ways he is like a nine-year-old. It's like having a perpetual child—and yes, sometimes it is really frustrating. I used to imagine Brett driving, going to prom at his high school, doing things like that. I don't think about that anymore, because it isn't going to happen."[13]

Society's Costs

There is no doubt that FAS is costly financially, too. Dr. Larry Burd, director of the Fetal Alcohol Center at the University of North Dakota School of Medicine, looked at the financial costs in caring for a victim of FAS. He estimated that in 2004 more than $4 billion would be spent on caring for all U.S. cases of FAS. The lifetime cost of a child diagnosed with FAS was estimated at $3 million.

The costs do not include just medical treatment but also residential care for FAS adults who are mentally retarded and a wide range of special education services. Burd also included the costs of treatment programs, since a large percentage of people with FAS will experience substance abuse problems. Court and incarceration costs were factored in for the estimated 60 percent of FAS victims who have trouble with the law.

"I think the numbers are probably low," says a Minneapolis health care worker. "I'm convinced that there are far more FAS adults and teens walking around today that have never been diagnosed. Teachers think they're lazy or slow, parents give up on them because the kids are hard to live with. Take a long hard look at the jails, the treatment programs, the halfway houses, the homeless shelters—I think we've got more FAS people in this country than we can imagine."

He says that the issue is not whether we should spend money on FAS. "It's a given," he says. "We have to—of course we do. But for every dollar we spend on treatment and help for the ones affected today, we should be spending two to find ways to keep women from drinking. If starting today, no pregnant woman would ever take another drink, FAS would disappear. There'd never be another FAS baby ever. Doesn't that make you stop and think?" [14]

Chapter 2

How Alcohol Does Its Damage

BY SHOWING THE connection between pregnant women drinking and the birth defects of their babies, Smith's and Jones's 1973 study proved that alcohol must be classified as a teratogen. From the Greek word meaning "monster maker," a teratogen is any substance that can harm the healthy growth of a fetus developing in its mother's body.

Alcohol was not the first teratogen discovered by scientists. Thalidomide, a prescription drug used as a sedative, was identified in 1961 as being harmful to unborn babies. It was then that scientists began noticing that thousands of babies born to women taking the drug were severely deformed, with missing or abnormal arms and legs. After that drug was banned, health officials began looking more closely at other chemicals or drugs used by pregnant women so that further tragedies could be avoided.

Studying Teratogens

A whole new branch of science emerged around the discovery of teratogens. Researchers study how certain toxins create problems in unborn children. They look at the amount of the toxin necessary to produce the effect and the timing of the exposure. For instance, some substances might be highly dangerous to a developing fetus at one stage yet relatively harmless at another stage.

Once alcohol was classified as a teratogen, scientists were eager to learn more about the damage it could do. How much alcohol was necessary to produce birth defects? Was there a safe amount of alcohol a pregnant woman could drink without endangering her child? Were there other effects of alcohol besides those noted in the 1973 study?

Since 1973, researchers in more than a dozen countries have conducted hundreds of experiments using laboratory animals. They studied how alcohol affects the bodies of adult rats as well as their unborn fetuses. They noted not only physical effects but also psychological and emotional ones. Much of what they have learned from these experiments has enabled them to understand how this disease works in humans.

As a result of habitual use of the sedative Thalidomide, this Swedish woman gave birth to a daughter with both arms missing.

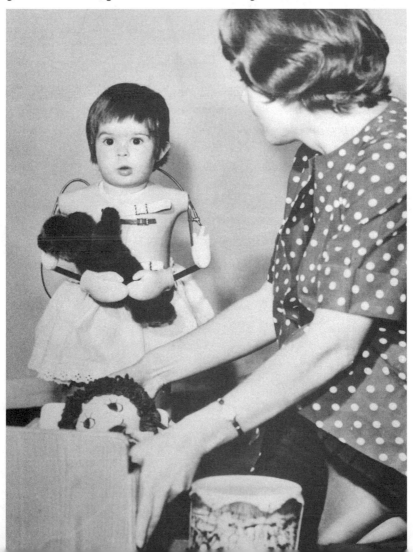

A Drunk Baby

When a woman is pregnant, everything she eats or drinks has an effect on the fetus inside her. The fetus lives within the placenta, an organ attached to her uterus. The placenta supplies the nutrients to the developing fetus through the umbilical cord. Until the baby is born, everything necessary for development and growth comes through the placenta.

When a pregnant woman drinks, the blood vessels in her stomach absorb the alcohol and transmit it directly into her bloodstream. Alcohol remains in the bloodstream until it is metabolized, or broken down by various chemicals in the body, especially in the liver. Meanwhile, the alcohol in the mother's system easily passes from her bloodstream to the placenta, where it affects the fetus. Scientists say that the level of alcohol in the fetus rises far above that of

A poster hung in a liquor store in North Carolina warns pregnant mothers of the serious dangers that alcohol poses to the fetus.

A Dirty Drug

New York Times *reporter Linda Carroll, in her article "Alcohol's Toll on Fetuses: Even Worse than Thought," explores the difficulty in determining just how alcohol affects unborn children.*

Further complicating matters is the question of how much alcohol it takes to cause harm. In the past few years, successive studies have shown an effect at increasingly lower levels. One study, published last year [in 2002], found a small but significant effect on average in children born to women who consumed just a drink and a half a week.

"We were surprised by this," said the lead author, Dr. Nancy Day. . . . "The children were in the normal range of growth . . . but if you compare them to children whose mothers didn't drink at all, they weighed less, were shorter, and had smaller head circumferences [indicating smaller brains]." . . .

Another factor making it difficult to tease out the impact of alcohol is its widespread effects on the developing brain and body. "Alcohol is a dirty drug," [expert Dr. James] West added. "It affects a number of different neurotransmitters, and all cells can take it up." Compare this with cocaine, Dr. West said, which is taken up by only one neurotransmitter.

It is also difficult to identify the effects of alcohol because a woman's drinking habits seem to make a big difference. Experts say it matters when a pregnant woman drinks, how often she drinks, and what her pattern of drinking is: whether she drinks small amounts daily, or periodically binges.

the mother. "As an adult, [the mother] has all kinds of . . . systems to decontaminate her from that substance," explains specialist Dr. Patricia Jett, "and the fetus [depending on its age and stage of development] may have none of that, or a small amount of that."[15]

Scientists have learned that the liver of an unborn baby can do less than 10 percent of the job of an adult liver. As a result, the mother's liver must do the work for both of them. To make things worse, the fluid within the placenta that cushions the fetus acts like a reservoir tank, holding the toxic alcohol for many hours at a time.

This means that the baby is intoxicated with a higher level of alcohol in its bloodstream than that of the mother, and for far longer. Research has shown that it can take three hours for a mother's liver to metabolize the alcohol of one beer from her unborn baby's body. Thus, the placenta has a higher concentration of alcohol than the mother's bloodstream. Writes one expert, "The baby in the womb becomes more drunk than its mother with every drink of liquor, wine, or beer she takes. By the time she feels tipsy and thus socially or physically compelled to refuse a refill, the child she carries could, in effect, have already passed out."[16]

Killing Cells

Once the alcohol is in the fetus's system, it can create a number of dangerous problems. It can dehydrate the delicate cells of the developing baby, disrupting and slowing their growth. In some cases, the cells die simply for lack of water.

The physical result of such damage to the cells was seen in experiments with rats. After feeding pregnant rats the equivalent of two or more drinks in a human being, scientists noted a wide array of physical abnormalities in the newborn baby rats. There were partially and malformed limbs, toes, eyes, ears, and various internal organs. Some of the rats were born dead, or with such extensive damage to their bodies that they did not survive for more than a few hours. These experiments produced the same problems in baby rats that human babies experience in severe cases of FAS.

Scientists were surprised to find that, in some cases, severe birth defects occurred in rats that had received alcohol on only one or two days of their pregnancy. For instance, pregnant rats that had two "binge" doses of alcohol on day seven of their pregnancy gave birth to babies with facial deformities, much like those in human children. Each of the baby rats had a narrow forehead and small head. They also had a thin upper lip and small eye openings.

Brain Damage

Research has shown that most of the physical problems caused by alcohol occur when a pregnant woman drinks in the first few months—often called the first trimester—of her pregnancy. That is the time when the bones and organs are being formed by growing cells. A woman who drinks in the second trimester of pregnancy

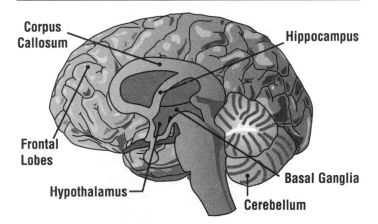

Alcohol Exposure and Brain Development

Corpus Callosum

Hippocampus

Frontal Lobes

Hypothalamus

Basal Ganglia

Cerebellum

Regions of the brain most affected by alcohol exposure in utero:

•Corpus Callosum (processes information between right brain and left brain)

•Cerebellum (motor control)

•Basal Ganglia (processes memory)

•Hippocampus (learning and memory)

•Hypothalamus (controls appetite, emotions, temperature, and pain sensation)

•Frontal Lobes (executive functions, impulse control, judgment)

has a higher risk of a premature delivery, or complications that may result in a stillborn baby.

Brain damage from alcohol, however, can occur anytime during a pregnancy, for the brain's development and growth continue for the whole nine months. Scientists know from rat experiments, as well as brain scans of children with FAS, that alcohol can interfere with the formation of the various parts of the brain. Alcohol constricts the blood vessels of the umbilical cord, cutting off the supply of oxygen to the fetus. When brain cells are deprived of oxygen, they die.

Some researchers have performed autopsies on children who died from FAS. They found that certain sections of the brain were far smaller than those in a normal child. In some cases, some sections of the brain were missing entirely. One of the most important areas of the brain that is susceptible to damage by alcohol is the corpus callosum. This is a thick band of about 250 million nerve fibers that ensure communication between the left and right hemispheres of the brain.

"You Never . . . Get Another Brain Cell"

There are many types of cells in the body, and many of them grow and reproduce throughout a person's life. However, most of the brain cells are produced when a fetus is developing in the uterus. And unlike other cells, brain cells are not replaced.

"A baby in utero [in its mother's uterus]—his brain . . . is perfectly smooth, like a little tennis ball—a little gray smooth surface," explains Dr. Barbara Kozol, a fetal alcohol syndrome specialist. "That baby . . . is growing 150 million brain cells a day!"[17]

Kozol says that when a pregnant woman drinks, she is depriving her baby of important cells it can never replace. The growing fetus has a once-in-a-lifetime chance for developing its brain, she explains, and alcohol can severely hinder that development. "Trying to grow his 150 million new brain cells, you have him in a toxic environment to begin with [because of the alcohol]," she says, "and you are also cutting off his oxygen supply. . . . By the time a typical baby is born, that brain growth is down to 10 million new cells a day. By the time he's six months old, that's it. You never, ever get another brain cell."[18]

Fetal Alcohol Syndrome – Brain Damage and Associated Behavior Problems

Executive functions of the prefrontal cortex	Effects of alcohol exposure on behaviors related to executive functions
• inhibition	• socially inappropriate behavior
• problem solving	• inability to figure out solutions
• sexual urges	spontaneously
• planning	• inability to control sexual impulses,
• time perception	esp. in social situations
• internal ordering	• inability to apply consequences from
• working memory	past actions
• self-monitoring	• difficulty with abstract concepts
• verbal self-regulation	• difficulty processing, storing, and/or
• motor control	retrieving information
• regulation of emotion	• needs frequent cues, requires policing
• motivation	by others
	• talks to self out loud, needs feedback
	• fine motor skills more affected than
	gross motor skills
	• moody, exaggerated emotions
	• apparent lack of remorse, needs
	external motivators

What Brain Damage Can Do

Not all brain damage results in the same problems. As FAS specialist Dr. Sterling Clarren notes, "It's clear that alcohol can pretty much do *anything* to the human brain to cause problems."[19] In most cases, the damage has an effect on the child's ability to learn. Experts estimate that the average IQ of individuals with FAS falls between 65 and 80, which translates as "mildly retarded" to "borderline normal." Some people with FAS, however, have been tested as high as 105, and as low as 15.

In addition to following the progress of children with FAS and observing their learning problems, researchers have done experiments with baby chicks with FAS. To create the condition, scientists injected alcohol into the air space in their eggs. The resulting chicks were born with limited ability to solve what should have been easy problems. In one experiment, the chicks were placed in a pen with a bowl of food. There was a piece of clear plastic in front of the food, so to reach it, the chicks needed to back up and go around a small barrier. The normal chicks had no trouble learning this; the FAS chicks, however, had difficulties even after being shown the correct way to the food several times. Many of them continued to walk into the plastic over and over, not learning from their mistakes.

Studies also show that brain damage can sometimes result in behavior problems. A number of studies indicate that brain damage from alcohol can make individuals more impulsive, acting without thinking through the consequences. Dr. Ronald Forbes found that many children with such brain damage may "show poor judgement and may repeat behaviors that have had bad outcomes in the past."[20]

"It's Like They're Pickled"

Even though scientists have been able to identify a number of symptoms of FAS in their observations and experiments, it is often very difficult for doctors to accurately diagnose the disease. After all, there is no blood test that can show evidence of FAS, nor is there an X-ray or other scan that will reveal it. Instead, doctors must rely on the presence of the characteristics of the most severe form of the disease: facial deformities, slow physical growth, and delayed learning, such as mental retardation.

One problem, say doctors, is that so many of the characteristics of FAS are not evident in newborn babies. Unless a doctor has reason to suspect that the mother has been drinking alcohol during her pregnancy, the signs of FAS could be missed or attributed to another cause. For example, limited learning ability could be a symptom of anything from Down syndrome to lead poisoning. As a result, only a very small percentage of babies are diagnosed with fetal alcohol syndrome when they are infants.

"It's rare," agrees Terry, a nurse in a northern Wisconsin hospital. "I've assisted in hundreds of births, but I've only seen two where the doctors have been confident in diagnosing FAS right after the delivery. One time, we had a woman in labor who had clearly been drinking when she was brought in to the delivery room, so that gave the doctor a reason to think about [FAS], you know? And the baby was in distress almost right away, [having] seizures, which were caused by withdrawal from alcohol.

"The other time, we had a newborn who had real obvious facial abnormalities. The mother had two other children who had been diagnosed [with FAS], so again, there was reason to give this baby a second look. Knowing that the mom was using [alcohol] was the key."[21]

Jeaneen Grey Eagle, the director of a drug and alcohol rehabilitation program on Pine Ridge Reservation in South Dakota, claims that occasionally the diagnosis can be as obvious as the smell of a newborn baby. "You see these women who are drunk every single day," she says, "and—you ask the doctors and nurses up at the hospital—there have been babies born whose skin, the whole baby, smells like wine. It's like they're pickled and the amniotic fluid [inside the placenta] is saturated with alcohol."[22]

A Tough Diagnosis

Unless doctors have a knowledge of the mother's alcohol use, or they see the baby experiencing the shakes or seizures resulting from alcohol exposure, they rarely have a reason to look for FAS in newborns. In fact, less than 3 percent of children diagnosed with FAS in the United States in 1999 (the most recent year for which such statistics are available) were under two months of age.

Even those with what some health professionals call "the FAS look"—protruding mouth, small eye openings, very thin upper lip—are not diagnosed unless the facial abnormalities are very obvious. "Except when a child is grossly dysmorphic [deformed]," notes Clarren, "[FAS] really cannot be diagnosed in newborns."[23]

A young boy suspected of suffering from FAS undergoes a dexterity test at a fetal alcohol syndrome clinic in Kansas.

Such was the case of Olivia, whose mother was drunk when she gave birth. Olivia was diagnosed as a newborn, and the damage done to her before birth was extensive. She was born with a cleft palate, malformed heart valves, only one functioning kidney, and defective ears. By age four she had endured four operations to repair some of her physical problems, but the brain damage she has cannot be repaired. She is unable to talk and is prone to fits of rage.

Her adoptive mother, Lisa, says that she feels sorry that her daughter can never overcome the brain damage caused by her birth mother's use of alcohol. "I'm sure she will never live a normal life because of the problems she has," Lisa says. "It's sad. It didn't have to be."[24]

"Everything Would Fall Apart on Friday Night"

Not every baby born with FAS has severe physical symptoms, however. Sherri, who drank while she was pregnant, knows this first-hand. She says she was not ignorant of the risks to her unborn child. In fact, she tried very hard to quit drinking when she learned she was pregnant. She could stop for only a few days at a time, however, and then she would binge, especially on weekends. "I stayed clean during the week, and everything would fall apart on Friday night," she remembers. "I didn't mean to do it. I told my doctor—I told him I was worried that this baby would be damaged.

"And when he was born, he was premature. That's one of the signs, you know. He was real small. I was so scared that he was going to be born with all the brain damage, the face like those kids have, right? And I asked the doctors—I was afraid to ask, but I did. And they told me, 'He's fine, he's fine.' But he wasn't fine. They just didn't see it until he was six months old."[25]

For Sherri's baby, and for many others with FAS, it was much easier to see there was a problem as time went by. Babies with FAS do not gain weight and grow as quickly as they should. They do not learn to sit up or to talk at the age when normal babies do.

"He Wouldn't Cry"

"For my son, I knew something was wrong when he wouldn't cry," Sherri remembers. "Tommy would lie in his crib, and he'd never try to turn over. He never seemed to do anything. One of my girlfriends who has a baby said, 'Oh, I'm so jealous 'cause you've got such a good baby—he's so easy to take care of.' But it wasn't a good thing. I'm the oldest of five kids, and I know babies are supposed to cry, like when they're hungry or they want to be picked up. Babies aren't supposed to be like Tommy was."

By the time her son was three months old, Sherri says, it was clear to her that there was something wrong. "He wasn't growing like he should have been," she says. "He didn't respond to toys or anything. He didn't care if you held him—really, that was the strangest thing. I felt like I needed to hold him more than he needed to be held. It didn't seem to make any difference to him. He hardly ever cried, but he hardly ever smiled, either."

Sherri says her baby did not have noticeable facial deformities. "His eyes seemed small," she says, "and his right eye always had a really droopy eyelid. But other than that, he looked OK to me. The doctor diagnosed him [with FAS] just after his first birthday. He was in the lowest percentile for height and weight. He wasn't anywhere close to being able to walk yet. Mostly because of the slowness of his development, and because of my drinking during the early and late part of my pregnancy, that's why the doctor diagnosed him when he did." [26]

The Key Piece of the Puzzle

David, age nine, was not diagnosed until he was eight years old. Lacking the physical signs of the disease, David was thought to be small for his age and a bit immature. "He had trouble in school," says his mother. "We were always told he didn't listen very well and that he didn't try very hard.

"David can be disruptive in class, too. We don't make excuses for that—it's the way he's always been. Every teacher has said that, even his preschool teacher. We always gave him time-outs when he was bad, but it didn't do much good, and I don't think it worked for his teachers, either. We had him tested for learning problems— attention deficit disorder [ADD] and that—because his teacher asked us to do it," she says. "I hoped that would be it, because there are strategies that can work with ADD kids. But it wasn't just ADD."

Darla says that finding out through her son's birth father that the mother had been an alcoholic helped them get a diagnosis for their son. "It put the pieces into place," she says. "All the behavior problems, the acting out. Knowing that his mother had been drinking heavily made all the difference for discovering what was the trouble for David." [27]

Not Easy

Experts in fetal alcohol syndrome know that many of the symptoms of FAS can be attributed to a range of other causes. Only when they know for certain that the child was exposed in utero to alcohol can they put it all together in a diagnosis.

"That's not as easy as it sounds, though," says one health professional. "There are so many instances where the mother's alcohol use isn't known to doctors. Lots of instances where babies who

Children with fetal alcohol syndrome like this girl often weigh less and are shorter than their healthy peers.

will later be diagnosed with FAS are put up for adoption by the mothers, and because of the privacy guaranteed in adoption, the mother's drinking isn't learned by the adoptive parents.

"In fact, a 2002 study indicates that of all the FAS babies born in the United States, only about 10 percent of them remain in the care

A Mother's Guilt

In Fantastic Antone Succeeds: Experiences in Educating Children with Fetal Alcohol Syndrome, *the editors include part of a memoir written by a woman named Anna, who was a recovering alcoholic. Anna had worried about the effects of her drinking on her unborn child. After her daughter's birth doctors had reassured her that the child was fine, but Anna realized later that, although the little girl did not have the physical abnormalities of FAS, she definitely had some of the brain damage caused by the disease.*

The nature of the grief that came with the realization of what happened to my daughter when I drank during pregnancy is unparalleled. It is profound, all-encompassing, mind-numbing, excruciating, ongoing, and unlike any other. . . . As I went through the grief process, I replayed, wept, became ill, raged, blamed, and feared. I turned yet again on myself, denigrating my own recovery and raging at a perverse deity. How hideous that I could recover and she would have possibly life-long struggles! Over and over I replayed "I love you, I hurt you, I can't kiss it and make it better. It's not fair for you." I read maybe the first word or sentence in a paragraph describing the effects, until my eyes refused to look after the first recognition of familiarity. . . . The "O my god, Omygods" came cyclically with each new awareness. I avoided reference as I furtively and fearfully worked through the process of discovery.

An adoptive father gives a bath to his three sons with FAS. Some couples adopt children without realizing they have the disease.

of their birth parents. That means there are a lot of babies with medical problems going through the adoption process."[28]

"If We Could Have Read About FAS"

Rob and Jean, who adopted a baby girl without realizing she had FAS, say that they would have preferred to know about their new daughter's condition beforehand. "It isn't that we'd think twice about adopting her," says Jean. "We love her. But it would have been so much better—for her and for us—if we could have read about FAS, learned about it.

"I think any medical information—especially regarding drug or alcohol use by the mother—should be provided [to adoptive parents]. Think of all the wasted time for adoptive parents who don't know why their children are the way they are. We could have made a better home for our daughter if we'd been prepared."[29]

Rob adds, "Of course, there are no guarantees in life, we are aware of that. If we'd had a biological child of our own, he or she could have been born with a disability, and we wouldn't have been prepared for that. But I agree with Jean—here was a situation where the birth mother's health wasn't explained to us."[30]

Other adoptive parents of children with FAS agree. They point to the high percentage of victims of FAS who have problems in school, who have trouble with the law, who become homeless, and who are more prone than others to abuse alcohol or drugs. Certainly, early diagnosis could mean that people with FAS could receive help to minimize such risks.

Embarrassed and Ashamed

For that to occur, however, doctors must get information about the mother's drinking history so that they can determine whether a diagnosis of FAS is reasonable. And even when the baby is not put up for adoption, doctors are often stymied by a lack of information about alcohol use.

"I'm not surprised that mothers don't always tell the doctors that they used [alcohol]," says one twenty-nine-year-old woman who asked to remain anonymous. "Embarrassment and shame are two reasons that come to mind. I drank even though I knew what might happen. I told myself that I wouldn't do anything to hurt the baby. But drinking is something—the only thing—that made me feel better when I was down.

"So I drank—sometimes a lot, sometimes just a little—all the way through my pregnancy. I'm very ashamed that I did," she insists. "I think about it every day, every single day. I see [my daughter] having trouble in school, being in the slow group for reading and math and everything else. She has trouble remembering things, has trouble making friends. She's got a lot of problems, and I know it's all my fault. All I can do now is try to be there for her, you know, all the time. I don't drink now. I've been clean since the day she was born, eight years ago. That doesn't make her better, but it can make me a better mom now."

She says that if she could tell pregnant women anything, she would advise them to be honest right away. "I know that it's real important for doctors diagnosing kids with FAS to have information about the mom's use of alcohol. They can't cure FAS, but they can help. Raising a child with FAS is tough, but there is support out there, once you tell people what's wrong."[31]

Chapter 3

Children with Fetal Alcohol Syndrome

W HETHER THEY HAVE already been diagnosed with FAS or not, children living with the disease experience a great number of challenges and problems that other children do not. Some of these challenges begin almost immediately after they are born; others do not appear until they are teenagers or adults.

"I Guess We'll Never Know"

Given the cause of the disease, it is not surprising that many children with fetal alcohol syndrome do not receive the best care from their birth mothers. Many of these women are alcoholics, and taking care of an infant—especially one with medical problems—is difficult.

Holly, for example, was neglected and abused during her sixteen months with her mother. She was often left alone in the house, tethered to her crib, while her mother went to a nearby town to drink. Because there was little money, the heat was often turned off, and Holly suffered severe frostbite on her legs during one of her mother's long absences.

"She had two strikes against her right away," says Holly's adoptive father. "She was born with FAS, and she was neglected." He says that he and his wife have frequently wondered whether Holly's emotional and behavioral problems would have been less severe if they had gotten her sooner. "How do you measure the effect of those long hours in a cold trailer on a baby? I guess we'll never know."[32]

"Like Having Fifty Kids at the Same Time"

Because they are so often neglected by their birth mothers, babies with FAS are often put into foster care until they can be adopted. One woman, who asked not to be named, says that her two youngest children—both with FAS—have been in foster care for the past six months.

"I want them back," she says. "I intend to get sober and stay that way so I can get them back. The baby was born with seizures, but he's lots better now. The older one is delayed, you know? He doesn't talk yet, he's real shy, real quiet. He's got some problems with his eyes, but he's going to get better real soon if he can get back to his mom, where he belongs. I don't want him living with strangers."[33]

Children with FAS who have been removed from their parents' home are often placed in the care of foster parents like this woman.

Though foster care is usually a safe transition for children who have been removed from their homes, it is not always a positive experience. Children with FAS are often frustrating for foster parents to deal with. "I've worked with kids [with FAS] who have been in four or five foster care situations before they hit their third birthday," says one child advocate. "The [foster] families complain that the kids won't listen to them, that they fight and have tantrums when they don't get their own way. One family who had three FAS children ages three, four, and six said it was like having fifty kids at the same time. None of them listened to rules or paid any attention when the foster parents talked."

She says she had total confidence in the nurturing abilities of that particular foster family, but admitted that other families might not be as patient. "Young children with the kinds of behavior we see with fetal alcohol syndrome can sometimes be really taxing. We see a lot of hyperactivity, a lot of inability to listen. I have to say that although it's unfortunate, it's not surprising to me when some families demand that we send the kids [with FAS] somewhere else."[34]

Pennies in the Toaster

Experts stress that the behavior of some children with FAS is not an indication that they are bad or are purposely misbehaving. Instead, they say, those with FAS are often impulsive, but unlike other children, they tend not to learn from mistakes and misbehavior. They repeat mistakes over and over, and seem baffled at their parents' exasperation. They also can seem oblivious to risk or danger.

One mother recalls when her adopted son, age three, first came to live with her. He put pennies in the toaster and cut holes in the water bed. Another adoptive mother, Karen, had similar experiences. "Destiny swallowed an open safety pin," recalls her adoptive mother, Karen. "She kicked her foot through a window. She pushed her brother down the stairs. She would keep eating until she threw up."[35]

One woman says that she and her husband were amazed at the number of problems their three-year-old son could cause within the span of an hour or two. "It was as though he had the endurance of three toddlers," she remembers. "He would purposely tip over the dog's water dish and I'd clean it up, and then he'd rush in and do it again. It wasn't typical toddler stuff. I wasn't expecting an angel, but it was over and over and over—he'd never get tired of doing the same thing.

"I'd sit him down and talk to him—explain that the dog would get thirsty if he kept spilling Rex's water. I gave him a time-out. Nothing worked, really. I could move the water dish, of course, but then he'd find something else to tip over or throw. I couldn't wait for my husband to come home in the afternoon, so he could experience the same fun I was having all day."[36]

"She . . . Couldn't Handle Transitions"

Many parents whose children have FAS report that the behavioral and emotional symptoms are especially noticeable when there is a change in routine. "Benny's never been able to handle it," says Denise. "Not as a toddler, and it's no better now. We learned a long time ago that you can't say, 'Tomorrow we're going to Grandpa's,' or 'Next week is your birthday.' Instead of giving him something pleasant to think about, to look forward to or whatever, it has the opposite effect. He gets stressed and really out of control."[37]

Holly's parents agree. "We'd notice it in the weeks before Christmas, when we'd get the holiday decorations out," says her mother. "Holly would be angry, and would lash out at us. It was as though she was mad that we weren't keeping her world the same every day. She simply couldn't handle transitions—going from one thing to something else. I think it was at these times when I understood how hard it was for her, and how much she was missing out on.

"She couldn't enjoy putting up the Christmas tree or looking at the lights. She couldn't think about making a present for her dad or helping us bake cookies. She couldn't even enjoy looking forward to Santa or presents, or visits from the relatives. It was all a nightmare for her."

Jean noticed that any new situation was stressful for her daughter, and the result would range from fear to fury. "I'll give you an example," she says. "If we were at home one morning and I needed to get to the grocery store, I really couldn't take Holly. I couldn't

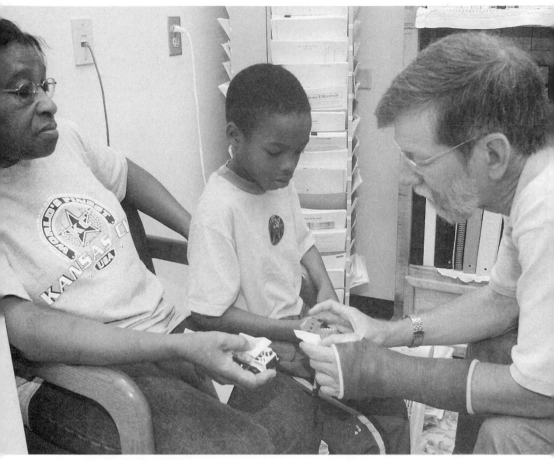

A psychologist meets with a boy with FAS and his grandmother. Therapy can help some children with the disease to cope with their emotional problems.

spring it on her—she would just get undone. She wasn't capable of making the switch from home to store.

"The couple of times we did go—when I had no choice but to take her with me—she was wild in the store. She screeched and screamed. I had no way of stopping it. And of course, all the other customers in the store would look at me—or my husband, when he took Holly to the store—like, 'What kind of parents are you?' A kid without FAS, you could ignore it, and the tantrum would stop in a couple of minutes. But not Holly. That control, it just wasn't in her." [38]

A Variety of Responses

For Holly, the usual response to a new situation was anger. "She'd lash out at us with her fingernails, really try to claw whoever was in her way," says her father. "I remember when we lived in Virginia, I was taking her to day care, and she was hitting me as hard

A teacher uses miniature bears to help a boy with fetal alcohol syndrome to count. Children with FAS often have learning disabilities.

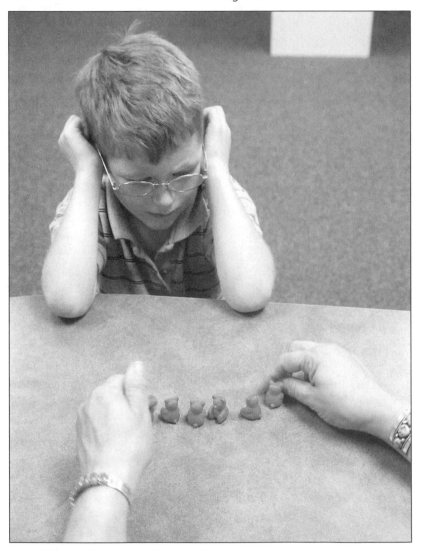

as she could, hitting my legs. I bent down to pick her up and she clawed my face. There was no reasoning with her." [39]

Not all children with FAS show their reluctance to new things by hitting. One toddler with FAS displayed her anger at her mother by holding her breath and fainting. This was, says her mother, "the ultimate sign to show her displeasure with changing from what was known and comfortable. The breath-holding spells were very scary, as Lisa would arch her back, turn blue, and pass out." [40]

Another child, John, had a physical ailment that he would use as a "weapon." He was born with a sensitive gag reflex, and when he was angry with his parents or could not get his way, he would make himself vomit.

School Problems

As children with FAS become old enough to attend school, they face new challenges. Many have a difficult time sitting still, concentrating, or being quiet at appropriate times. And many school-age children with FAS have trouble with subjects such as social studies or mathematics.

"Instruction that is not in the here and now—you're going to lose kids with any fetal alcohol effects," says one counselor. "If they can't see it, touch it, whatever, they will have a very hard time understanding what it is." [41]

One woman says that her six-year-old daughter with FAS had the most trouble in arithmetic. "The teacher was using brightly colored beanbags to show the kids the idea of adding," she explains. "I think Michaela understood it when the beanbags were involved, but making the connection with the numeral five standing for the five beanbags was like a foreign language for her. She did learn it eventually, but it was a struggle that went on for more than a month, and that's with her dad and I helping her every night. Her teacher was very patient, but I could tell she was running out of strategies to teach Michaela this abstract idea that the other students were grasping so easily." [42]

Homeschooling

The difficulty some children have in keeping up with their classmates is one reason some families decide to homeschool their children with

FAS. Jan Hinde, whose son Jeffrey was diagnosed with FAS, was told that his IQ would most likely be between fifty and sixty-five, based on early childhood screening tests. She knew from researching the disease that school would likely be an overwhelming experience for him.

Like most parents, Hinde wanted her son to succeed more often than to fail, and she encourages other parents who want their child with FAS to do well to consider the difficulty of a regular school setting. "If you know Jeffrey has difficulty sitting still," she asks, "then why would you take him to some place where you know he must sit quietly? If you know a child cannot act appropriately or within an acceptable range in a certain type of situation, why choose to humiliate him?"[43]

Hinde found that Jeffrey was able to do more than experts had predicted, because she could teach her son at his own pace and give him full attention. She learned how to tailor the lessons to the ways he learned best. The key, she discovered, was to work on teaching one thing at a time, whether it was to write the letter "S" or to learn to sit still for more than five minutes.

Jeffrey accomplished much more than anyone had expected. His language skills, which had been his weakness, improved, as did his social skills. "When we first started," Hinde recalls, "Jeffrey would throw objects in frustration if he did not understand or was asked to do something he did not want to do at that time. A teacher with twenty children in a classroom would find it difficult to cope with such episodes—other children could get hurt. A mother can lovingly insist that he perform the task without throwing anything."[44]

Success at a Price

Many children with FAS cannot handle the structure and pace of a regular classroom, but some can—although parents say that it is often a tough battle. Sally Caldwell, a special education teacher whose adopted son Antone was diagnosed as an infant with FAS, says that perhaps he has had success because his brain damage was not as severe as the physical damage caused by his mother's alcohol abuse.

Homeschooling a Child with FAS

By fourth grade, writes Linda Heinen in her article "Homeschooling a Child with Fetal Alcohol Syndrome," her son had been left behind by other students his age. Her decision to homeschool him has resulted in more realistic goals as well as more appropriate lessons.

Our son was happily attending an Independent Christian school until he was in the fourth grade. However, it became apparent that his good buddies were steadily outgrowing him and the gap in abilities was ever widening. Soon he became very unhappy as he realized that he was different and could not do the things that they were doing. So I began homeschooling him, and the lad became more cheerful.

That year I became his scribe and wrote out his oral answers. We even wrote out his stories, which were quite well told. However, the following year we had to go back to basics as he was not using phonics to read, but had begun to guess at what he saw. He was also losing the ability to spell even the simple words he once knew. . . .

Science this year is a unit study on the horse. Besides learning about horses we are reading real novels such as *King of the Wind, The Black Stallion,* and so on. Perhaps he will learn enough so that he will be able to train a pony and do it well enough to have a career with horses.

Math was a mystery for him years ago, and we will be happy if he learns how to buy food and clothing within his budget when he is older.

Even so, she knew she could not have the same expectations for Antone's schooling as other parents whose children do not have FAS. As do many children with FAS, Antone needed predictability and structure, and tended to fall apart emotionally when those things were not part of the school day. Antone's success—receiving above-average scores on his school's achievement tests—is that much more admirable, for Antone's accomplishment was definitely not easy. His mother says that she can see that the effort he has put into school has been stressful. As each week goes by, she says, "staying in control becomes out of his reach":

> On Monday, he comes home from school and is willing, focused, responsive, affectionate, sympathetic, able to work and complete tasks independently. By Friday, he is resistive, scattered, inattentive, unable to follow even simple, single command instructions . . . and is failing at any attempt to use techniques that normally help him focus. Sharp, repetitive sounds erupt from him at inappropriate times. . . . Like a stuck record, he repeats phrases and loses his train of thought.[45]

They Thought They Could Change Her

Some parents say that it is when their children are old enough to attend school that they truly understand the extent of the disease. One mother claims that she always believed that her daughter would be somewhat normal, even with FAS. "I just believed that with enough structure, and love, and support, we could change the bad things that were going on inside her," she says. "But as she turned five, then six, and seven, and still seemed incapable of sitting still long enough to hear a story or do some fingerpainting, it dawned on me that it might never happen."[46]

Michael Dorris, whose book *The Broken Cord* describes his adopted son Adam's struggle with FAS, had a similar realization when looking back on Adam's school experience. He, too, had believed that with the right motivation and personal help, Adam could be a good student, or at least keep up with most of the class. "I sometimes had the fantasy," he writes, "that if I could penetrate the fog that surrounded Adam's awareness and quickly explain what was what, he would be fine. He was just slightly out of focus."[47]

However, in retrospect, Dorris knows that his goals of having Adam be a "normal" boy were wishful thinking on his part:

> At no time in his life could Adam, by any stretch of the imagination, read a map or comprehend the principles of geometry.

In eight years [of school] he never once received so much as a telephone call or an invitation from a "friend." He never stayed in his seat for more than a few minutes unless he was supervised. . . . In grade after grade, Adam was working at the same level on exactly the same tasks.[48]

Michael Dorris wrote a critically acclaimed book called The Broken Cord *that details his family's experience raising a son with fetal alcohol syndrome.*

Adam at School

In this excerpt from his book The Broken Cord: A Family's Ongoing Struggle with Fetal Alcohol Syndrome, *Michael Dorris looks back on his son Adam's school years and realizes that, because at the time nothing was known about FAS, his teachers were not able to recognize Adam's disabilities.*

When Adam was young, people fell in love with him and with the idea of him. He was a living movie-of-the-week hero, an underdog who deserved a happy ending. On top of that, he had good manners, an appealing face, me to broker and block for him. He was the only full-blood Indian most people at his school had ever met. His learning problems at first appeared so marginal, so near to a solution. With just the smallest nudge they would pass over the line into the normal range. Every good teacher, every counselor, every summer camp director Adam encountered in grade school and high school viewed him as a winnable challenge and approached his education with initial gusto and determination. He teetered in his ability so close to the edge of "okay" that it seemed impossible that, with the proper impetus, he would not succeed. I understood this conviction perfectly and succumbed to it for fifteen years. . . .

The fact was, improvement was hard to come by and even harder to sustain once it had appeared. Reviewing those end-of-the-year teacher reports, it is not clear that in grade after grade Adam was working at the same level on exactly the same tasks. Every year he started fresh, showed promise up to a point, then couldn't take the next step.

Tougher Going in Adolescence

Regardless of whether children with FAS are schooled at home or in a classroom, their parents and teachers can find ways to help them learn. However, as those children grow into adolescents, those same strategies do not always work as they did before.

"It's being teenagers," says one counselor. "It matters not one bit if you have FAS or cerebral palsy, or cancer, or none of those things. They are growing and changing on the inside and outside and they're confused. The people they used to talk to—their parents—are no longer worthy of conversation. For the teenager with FAS, though, the differences between them and their peers are more pronounced. They feel—and are—different. And that, to any teenager, is frightening." [49]

The differences are evident in the classroom. Whereas elementary grades focus on basics, which can be frustrating enough for a child with FAS, junior high and high school focus on more theoretical, abstract learning. That, for many students with FAS, is almost impossible.

"My son, who at age fourteen functioned at an eight-year-old level, couldn't understand anything his teachers said," remembers Anne, his mother. "It wasn't so noticeable in elementary school, but [in] junior high everything just seemed to fall apart for him. Brett would come home and I'd ask him what he needed to work on, and he didn't know—didn't know where to begin, I guess. He'd cry and throw things. Tantrums we hadn't seen in years came back. I know it was all terribly hard for him, and that's the reason for the acting out. It was as if we had suddenly moved to a different country, where they spoke a new language.

"It was frustrating, to say the least. Brett began to hate school, and talked about how angry he felt at all of his teachers. He believed they hated him, and he insisted that he hated them right back. I can't tell you how hard it was to see the transformation in our son. This was a boy who loved school when he was younger—even when he had a hard time learning a particular thing. His counselor at the [junior high] school was sympathetic. She told us that everything speeds up in junior high. She said it was hard on kids without disabilities, too. I guess Brett just couldn't keep pace." [50]

"The System Set Him Up for Failure"

Ryland, at age thirteen, had a similar experience. "He had a different teacher for every class," explains Mary Lou, his mother, "different expectations for each class, a different schedule for every day, and three different combinations to memorize—one for his hall locker, another for his gym locker, and a third for his bicycle. Between classes students jammed the hallways, which upset Ryland, who is [like many people with FAS] sensitive to touch." Mary Lou believes that by its very nature, junior high was not feasible for Ryland. "The system set him up for failure," she says.

Though some days he was able to do well, pleasing his teachers and making friends, he could not sustain that level for too long. "Doing everything well all the time became so exhausting for him that at home he pestered his brother and his sisters verbally and physically, became agitated, fought with neighbor kids, and couldn't focus on anything."

Ryland's frustrated outbursts were aimed at his teachers and classmates, too. He began fighting in the hallways and talking back to teachers and failing in his schoolwork. He was eventually sent to special education classes, which he interpreted as a failure. "In the school's sink or swim program," says Mary Lou, "Ryland sank."[51]

The Wrong Friends

Because of problems like the ones encountered by Ryland, it is not uncommon for teens with FAS to struggle with friendships, too. They might be viewed unkindly by their peers, and even those classmates who had once been friendly may find themselves unwilling to continue such friendships. "That was hard," says one father whose son complained that he had no friends. "He never really had lots of friends, but there were kids he knew from church and from the neighborhood who at least talked to him back in grade school.

"But that changed right off the bat when seventh grade started. No one wanted to admit they knew him. I don't blame the other kids, not really. I know he can act silly and loud. He hugs people—it's just what he does, right? But to a seventh grade boy trying to look cool at the bus stop, that's not the best thing that could happen—having another seventh grade boy come up and hug you."[52]

Interaction with peers is typically difficult for adolescents with fetal alcohol syndrome. As a result, they can be made to feel socially isolated.

When teens with FAS feel discouraged and socially excluded, they can be targeted by others—either teased or manipulated to do reckless or inappropriate things. Not understanding that what his "friends" are telling him to do is actually wrong, a teen with FAS may agree to do it.

"Friends Don't Use Each other"

Tommy, a teenager with FAS, had trouble with the wrong type of friends in junior high. "He was the butt of a lot of jokes," says Earl, his father. "He is a very trusting kid, and that's one of his strong points. But it can be a weakness, too, because some of his classmates took advantage of that side of him.

"One of the most painful things that happened was during his second year of high school, when some boys convinced him that a girl at school wanted to go out with him. Well, she didn't at all—they'd just made that up to watch Tom ask her out. He didn't understand—even when the girl rejected him and the guys laughed. I tried to explain it to him, but he kept saying, 'Dad, she really liked me, she really liked me.'

"Stuff like that is hard for parents. You want to protect him, you know, because, he's your kid. We tell him, 'Friends don't use each other like that—those guys weren't really being your friends.' But you don't want to make him feel like no one likes him. You also don't want to make it look to the other kids like you're fighting your sixteen-year-old's battles for him. That's no good, either."

No Easy Answers

Earl says that while Tommy has made a lot of progress with his studies, social relationships have been hard. "He has adult friends, people he knows that understand that he needs a little help. I hope that as he gets older, he can meet friends his own age, too. It's hard for him, hard for us as his parents. There aren't really any easy answers. I guess we just have to trust we're doing the right things."[53]

Chapter 4

Adults with Fetal Alcohol Syndrome

P ARENTS OF CHILDREN with FAS often worry about what will happen when their children become adults. Fetal alcohol syndrome is not something that a child outgrows. Although some of the physical symptoms—especially facial signs of the disease—often diminish after puberty, the mental and behavioral abnormalities do not.

"It's Kept Us Up Nights"

"Just the idea of Tommy living on his own is unimaginable," says Earl, his father. "He has a heart of gold, he trusts everyone, and he's the friendliest guy you'd ever meet. But he has no common sense—or at least what I would call common sense. He has no concept of time passing, he isn't careful with his possessions.

"One of the things my wife and I worry about most is what will happen to Tom if we weren't around. He'd need to be in some residential facility or something, a group home maybe. I don't know. It's kept us up nights, thinking about it. My wife and I are in our sixties, so it's something you think about, you know?"[54]

Other parents whose children are victims of FAS voice similar fears. Like Earl, many of them worry about how their children will earn a living or where they will live when—or if—they strike out on their own. "How long are we the primary caregivers?" wonders one woman. "We have four adopted kids, and they've all gone off and gotten jobs, apartments, whatever. They'll get married and have kids, probably. But our youngest—she's the one with FAS— I don't believe those things are in the cards for her."[55]

This couple adopted nine children, some of which have FAS. The children will have to learn to cope with their disease as they mature into adulthood.

Getting a Job

The first step in independence is often finding a job, and this can be difficult for many individuals with FAS. This is not because many FAS-affected people are retarded. There are actually many mentally retarded people in the U.S. workforce, especially people with Down syndrome. The problem, say experts, is that many job programs for mentally disabled people in the United States are designed for those with Down syndrome. People with that condition tend to be more easygoing and relaxed, and often make good, dependable workers in jobs focusing on repetitive tasks, such as assembly-line work. However, as reporter Elizabeth Rosenthal found, "Parents and health professionals describe the alcohol-affected [those with FAS] in very different terms: impulsive, unable to learn from mistakes, undisciplined, showing poor judgement, distractable, uninhibited."[56]

Jean, whose daughter is now an adult, agrees with such terms. "She has not been able to keep any of the jobs she's had," she says. "She is not retarded. She is brain damaged, and that's exhibited by her impulsiveness and poor judgment. 'Docile' is the last word I'd use to describe my daughter. To be honest, if she were more docile, she would probably be a better worker, because she'd get along better with people."

Jean explains that the jobs Holly has had—and lost—have involved working with the public, such as being a cashier in a grocery store. "She can do the job," says Jean, "but then she gets

Difficulty at Work

In her book Fetal Alcohol Syndrome: A Guide for Families and Communities, *FAS expert Ann Streissguth recounts the discouragement of a young man with FAS hoping to succeed at his first paying job.*

Jack was thrilled to get his first paying job as a young adult. He was willing and eager to do a good job. He'd done volunteer work in an office and had responded well to the experience. Therefore, his subsequent work as a busboy at a busy restaurant seemed to be well within his capabilities. . . . To his chagrin, he had great difficulty knowing which tables he was supposed to clear.

At this restaurant, the tables to be cleared by the busboys were identified by the waitresses' names: "Jane's table needs clearing." Not only did Jack have difficulty recalling the waitresses' names from day to day, but even when he learned that Jane was the one with braids, he didn't recognize her on a day when she didn't braid her hair. Jack got increasingly discouraged and gradually just stopped showing up for work.

mad—either at a customer or one of her fellow employees. It doesn't have to be for an important issue. It can be anything. She's got a real explosive temper. That's Holly—she's always been that way, and she hasn't learned. Maybe she never will. I don't think she's bad, she just cannot control herself when she gets irritated."[57]

Change Is Hard

Transitional situations are as difficult for adults with FAS as they are for children with the disease. At work, changes are often the reason why some FAS adults have trouble with their fellow employees, customers, and supervisors.

Even minor changes can be stressful for those with FAS. One woman says that her daughter called her from work one morning in tears. "She had been working at the discount drugstore for

A developmentally disabled worker stocks a grocery-store storeroom. Adults with FAS find themselves challenged to deal with the stresses of the workplace.

two months," she says. "It had been going fine, no real problems. She worked the cash register, and sometimes stocked shelves. But she was upset because they wanted the employees to wear red smocks, you know, over their blouses. And she was in tears, literally. She was used to wearing the white blouse and dark skirt, and this was a change she wasn't ready for. No one can understand this stuff if you've never had a kid with [FAS]."[58]

Sometimes a person's difficulty with change on the job can be overcome. Bert, a young man with FAS serving time in prison, was given a promotion at work but did not want it. He enjoyed the job he had, even though it paid less and was more repetitive. When his supervisors told him one morning to report to another part of the prison, Bert panicked, fearing that he would not be able to do another job.

It was not until a corrections officer named Jim intervened that the situation was resolved. Jim knew something about FAS, and realized that Bert needed to feel that he had a choice in the matter. He also knew that Bert might succeed at the new job if he had the opportunity to learn it gradually. Jim explained to Bert that he could have his old job if he wanted it, but he might want to give the new one a try. If he still preferred working in the laundry, he could go back. Knowing he had the choice to keep his routine intact, Bert was able to relax, and eventually accepted his promotion.

Needing More Supervision

Michael Dorris's son Adam did not have the same success on the job as Bert. Adam tended to be easygoing and eager to please. However, as Dorris found out when Adam got his first job as an adult—an outdoor maintenance man at a large park—his disabilities prevented him from doing the work. Just as when Adam was a student, he was unable to stay on track without constant supervision:

> It was the same old story—consistent with his school performance for twelve years. . . . If someone in authority stood over Adam and told him each thing to do, every day, he would follow instructions. The minute the person left, however, the minute he was on his own, he became distracted, wandered off, lost

interest. . . . On more than one occasion, Adam attempted to avoid a work assignment by hiding behind a tree.[59]

Not surprisingly, when Dorris helped his son apply for the job again the following summer, Adam was not rehired. At first Dorris was unhappy, feeling that Adam's supervisors had not given him a fair chance. "I ranted and raved to Louise [his wife]," he writes. "[I] threatened to sue, to expose what seemed to me overt injustice."[60] As time passed, however, Dorris was able to see that Adam was not equipped to handle a job like that. The disabilities caused by FAS were too severe for him to succeed at that time without the complete supervision he required.

"The Thing That Makes Me Happiest"

Not every adult with FAS has difficulty holding a job. Depending on the nature and severity of the disability, and the level of support from parents or advocates, a person with FAS can be a very good employee. Dave, age twenty-five, is a good example.

He has worked in a local restaurant for three years, which experts say is an exceptional achievement. Dave says that it has not always been easy. He has a hard time dealing with stress when the restaurant becomes busy. But, he says, thanks to cooperation between an understanding employer, his therapist, and coworkers, he has been able to keep doing his job, and that makes him very proud.

"The thing that makes me happiest right now is work," says Dave. "I have a few close friends at work. I try to help them out as much as I can and they help me out as much as they can. It makes work easier for me in terms of stress. . . . Sometimes it gets too busy, and I can't keep up. Then I have to ask someone for help to get back on track. Most of the time I work by myself, but I need someone else to help me get everything done."[61]

Pitfalls of Living Alone

Besides finding a job, leaving the security of their parents' home can be very difficult for individuals with FAS. Some of the difficulty includes handling important tasks on their own, such as

A young girl with fetal alcohol syndrome prepares lunch for herself. Such independent behavior will benefit her in her adult life.

preparing meals. For Adam, it was remembering to take the medication necessary to control his seizures (one of the effects of FAS) and dressing appropriately for the weather.

After Adam had been on his own for several weeks, his father visited him at his job at the bowling alley, and was concerned by the young man's appearance. He learned that Adam had not been careful about taking his medicine during the day and, as a result, had suffered a seizure. More obvious was his son's apparent disregard for hygiene:

> He had not shaved or washed his face in some time. I did not criticize his choice of clothing: a torn T-shirt in frigid November,

a shabby pair of sweat pants, worn obviously without under-
wear, the ravaged running shoes I had begged him to discard
weeks before. The nails on his fingers were long and jagged,
his teeth not clean, his hair unbrushed. [62]

"He Depends on Others"

Many adults with FAS struggle with other aspects of independent
living, such as adhering to a schedule. "This is where our son has
trouble," says one woman. "He doesn't do well with the concept
of time. We've never been able to get him to hang on to a watch,
and even at home where we have clocks in the kitchen and on the
mantle, he doesn't notice. Time is too abstract a concept, and his
teachers in special ed have told us that.

*A caretaker watches as an adult with FAS prepares dinner at a group home
for developmentally disabled people in California.*

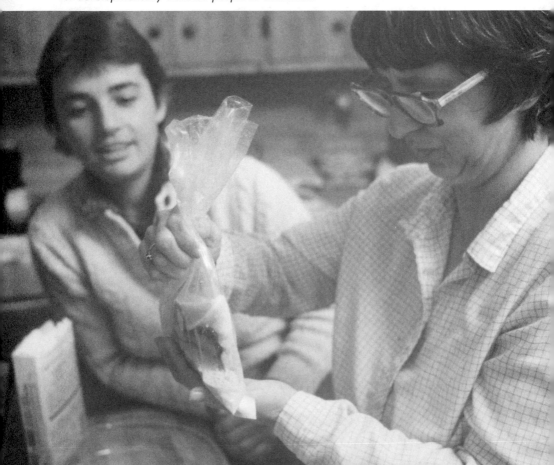

"So when he is on his own, he depends on others to tell him what to do. We've got a big family, and we have always lived in a small town, so that's OK for now. There's always someone around to remind him to come home for dinner, or to go lock up [the dogs' pen, part of his job as a veterinarian's helper]. On his own, though—away from home—I think someone would have to be with him."[63]

Many parents of children with FAS agree that the one thing that seems to be critical for their adolescent and adult children to get along is structure. And it is not only a matter of meals and work being consistent, either. "My daughter lives in an assisted living home for adults with disabilities," says one woman. "She has a hard time when things change. When the woman next door moved out and a new woman moved in, it was hard on her. It wasn't that she was close friends with the gal that moved. She just didn't want things to change. That made her life hard for a week or two."[64]

Too Trusting? Too Generous?

Parents of individuals with FAS often worry that their children will get into trouble because of their trusting attitude. Because it is common for those with FAS to take people at face value, it is easy for others to take advantage of them.

Bill, who was diagnosed with FAS, had obtained funding for a nice place to live. Whether he was trying to make friends or simply help less fortunate people, Bill began hanging around a local teen shelter, offering to let them stay at his home. Unfortunately, the arrangement backfired. "His apartment quickly turned into a flophouse," explains FAS expert Jim Slinn, "as those he invited to stay brought other friends and then held disruptive parties that created unhappy neighbors and an angry landlord. . . . Eventually, he was evicted, labeled as 'trouble.'"[65]

Dealing with Loneliness

Some parents claim that one of the hardest things for their adult children with FAS to deal with is loneliness. "They feel different all along," says one mother. "In school my daughter was not popular by a long shot. She had no friends in her class. She hung around with younger kids sometimes, and in high school, it was much the same. She had her family, but we were her social life.

"And now it's the same. She's older, she has a part-time job, but very little else in her life. I know she'd like a friend, or even a group of people from work or whatever that she could hang out with. But it's not something she's ever been able to handle. She's emotionally about eight years old—in the body of a twenty-four-year-old." [66]

Ironically, many FAS victims turn to alcohol or drugs as a way of easing the loneliness they feel. For them, drinking is very dangerous, for their impulsiveness and poor decision-making skills can make it difficult to control the use of alcohol. "Our daughter was diagnosed with fetal alcohol syndrome when she was ten," says one South Dakota woman. "And she had started drinking by age twelve. I think for her, drinking is all about having friends, and doing what her friends want to do.

"She's been in treatment six times already. It seems for a while that she is going to stop using, but within a month or so, she gets back with her old friends and starts up again. She just can't think for herself. We've told her how bad alcohol can be. She knows all that. She knows it was her mom's drinking that is responsible for her problems today. But she just can't walk away from those friends." [67]

FAS and Parenthood

Another concern parents have for their adult children with FAS is whether they will become parents. One Sioux health worker says that it is more than a concern, it is a monumental worry.

"We're having a lot of trouble with parents who have no idea of how to take care of kids," she says. "It's not only that they're young, it's that they are alcohol-affected. They can't keep a job, they can't make decisions on where to live, how to pay rent. They don't know how to manage money, or how to keep track of time. And yet they have two, three, four kids. I'm not passing judgment," she insists. "It's not that they are bad people. But they haven't got the ability to care for a little child."

She says that parents with FAS probably mean well but cannot organize themselves well enough to make good decisions. "I've had

Lifelong Consequences

In the following excerpt from Jane Kwiatkowski's Buffalo News *article "Challenged at Birth," she interviews experts at the Pregnancy Risk Network and Erie County Council for the Prevention of Alcohol Abuse, who maintain that FAS creates problems for victims throughout their whole lives.*

The long-term consequences of fetal alcohol syndrome can haunt a lifetime, said [Sandra] Gangell, program coordinator for Pregnancy Risk Network. From the infant who fails to thrive to the hyperactive preschooler and the impulsive adolescent—alcohol's impact at birth means significant challenges through life.

"You look at these children or adults as being impulsive, poor decision makers, liars, troublemakers, class clowns. They don't behave properly," Gangell said. "A lot of women are sexually taken advantage of because they finally see somebody liking them."

"They try and hold down a job and they just can't handle it. They can't plan and schedule," [expert Helen] Weinstein said. "Often if they're on any kind of public assistance, they get labeled as noncompliant because they have difficulty with anything abstract, which includes time. Time is very hard for them."

Meanwhile, the undiagnosed are left to muddle through life, their difficulties in school attributed to poor behavior, poor parenting, or manipulation. Rarely will the mother identify herself as being an alcohol abuser.

cases where parents will leave their child with the grandparents one evening. But they don't come home. They go off for a week, or a month. They don't think about what that does to a child, or to the grandparents, for that matter. A lot of times, grandparents or other family members without FAS will end up raising the child."[68]

"It Breaks Your Heart"

That situation is happening to Tom and Louise, both in their sixties. Their daughter Karen was diagnosed with FAS when she was in grade school. An IQ test revealed that she was marginally retarded, and although she attended special education classes, school proved too hard for her.

"She's basically a good girl," says Louise, "but she's been drinking for the last seven years. She went to treatment in Iowa once and Minnesota once, but she can't stay off the booze. She drank during her own pregnancy—both times—and her two kids have problems. Our social worker says second- and third-generation kids with FAS isn't unusual."

Louise says that her grandchildren, ages four and eighteen months, are both retarded, and one is blind. "It breaks your heart to see them," she says. "What can we do? What can anyone do? Those kids will grow up, and—I hate to say it—they might go down the same path as Karen. We worry about that. Right now, we've got the kids, we're raising them while [Karen] is in treatment again. But who knows

Many women with FAS, like this pregnant alcoholic at a group therapy session, drink during pregnancy and give birth to children with the disease.

what will happen then. You hope for the best, you know, but I think it's one of those situations where it seems like there's no answer."[69]

Trouble with the Law

Because of the trouble many individuals with FAS have with decision making and impulsiveness, they are at a much higher risk for breaking the law. Some experts believe that as many as half of the people in U.S. prisons and jails may be victims of FAS. At least 60 percent of adults or adolescents diagnosed with FAS have had trouble with the law. Even more troubling, 42 percent of adults or adolescents with FAS have been in jail or prison—more than have been in organized mental health programs such as group homes or supervised job training.

Many experts say that because they are retarded or socially immature, such individuals do not always understand that the behavior of which they have been accused is wrong. They may go along with others stealing a car, for example, because they want to fit in. "If someone told Tom they'd be his friend if he held up the First National Bank, he'd do it," says Tom's father, Earl. "He knows right from wrong at the time we talk about it, but once the subject is over, he doesn't remember."

He says that Tom has shoplifted several times, and once was charged with damaging a woman's car. "We're not completely sure why he did that," says Earl. "Basically, he keyed the car, scratched the whole side. He told us no one told him to do it, but I don't buy that. He's not a mean kid or a vindictive one. The woman is a teacher at the high school, and my guess is someone dared Tom to damage the car. He did, and he got in trouble for that."[70]

"Being Incarcerated Isn't Going to Work"

Many advocates for people with FAS insist that jail or prison is not the best solution. For one thing, notes psychologist Judith Kleinfeld, fetal alcohol syndrome is often a puzzle to the legal system in the United States. While there are guidelines for dealing with people who have psychiatric problems that can be easily diagnosed, or those with a visible disability such as Down syndrome, there is nothing in place for those with FAS.

People with fetal alcohol syndrome are at an elevated risk for breaking the law and being incarcerated in a prison like this one in Florida.

"The problem is that it's not easy to diagnose," says one counselor. "Some kids have the facial deformities, while others don't. Some are retarded, others aren't. [Not having] . . . a way to diagnose FAS accurately in all these cases throws the system off. It's often so hard to see, so many offenders with FAS get treated like everyone else.

"And that isn't good," he says, "because being incarcerated isn't going to work. These offenders won't really understand what they've done to get there. And without understanding that, how can they be rehabilitated? They won't be—that's the thing. There's every reason to believe that many people [with FAS] who commit crimes will repeat the offense again and again, just because they don't understand what it is that has happened."[71]

Changing Expectations

There are plenty of ways that life with FAS presents challenges to those who suffer from it, as well as to their families. And it seems that there are fewer happy endings than disappointing ones. Even so, many parents of FAS children say that there are many successes, too. The key, they say, is learning to change their expectations.

"I define success for each of my children quite differently," says Jan, an adoptive mother of eight children with FAS. "Success may mean finishing things some of the time. It means hitting a punching bag instead of a person. Success means knowing who you are, accepting yourself, and understanding that everyone has handicaps. For someone with FAS, success means knowing that these goals are worth striving for, not someone else's unreachable line in the sand." [72]

Another parent agrees completely. "If it takes my son twice as long to get his education as everybody else, hey, at least he got there," he says. "There are a lot of disappointments in Tom's life. He'll always need help—from us, from his counselor, whatever. My wife and I know that. But I can celebrate with him the accomplishments in his life, too. They may not mean much to other families, but we know different." [73]

Chapter 5

Making Strides Against FAS

U NLIKE OTHER DISEASES or disorders, fetal alcohol syndrome is not going to be cured with a medicine or prevented with a vaccine. Nor is there a mystery to be solved as to why babies are born with the effects of alcohol exposure. Even though there are no magic potions to prevent or cure FAS, however, there is a great deal of work being done, both to reduce the number of people affected by FAS and to improve the quality of life for those already struggling with the disease.

Drinking on the Rise

The statistics that are most alarming to FAS experts are those that show that drinking among pregnant women has actually increased since 1991. In some areas of the United States, the increase is significant. One doctor from Buffalo, New York, is aware that prenatal drinking is on the rise. "Maternal drinking is increasing not only in Buffalo, but across the country," he says. "Data shows that one in twenty women drink during pregnancy. These women have a drink every couple of days; three percent drink at risk levels."[74]

A social worker in Vandalia, Indiana, says that she, too, sees an increase in prenatal drinking and the incidence of FAS there. "We have been seeing more of this, and one reason is because we are starting to learn more about what the warning signs are. People need to know about the dangers of FAS. We are still finding doctors out there who are telling women that it's okay to have a few drinks during pregnancy. But it's not."[75]

The lack of leadership by obstetricians, doctors who treat pregnant women, is worrisome to many experts of fetal alcohol syndrome. A 2002 study by Virginia Commonwealth University found that of eighty-one medical textbooks being used around the country, only fourteen of them urge doctors to advise their patients not

Recent statistics reveal that drinking among pregnant women is actually on the rise. Here, a teen woman in her third trimester drinks a beer.

to drink during pregnancy. "Women need to know that when they drink, their baby is drinking, too," notes an editorial in the New Orleans *Times-Picayune*. "That's a pretty simple message, but it won't get across unless the doctors who treat pregnant women know it, too."[76]

Alcohol Is "the Root of What We Struggle With"

The increase in prenatal alcohol use is especially high on Indian reservations throughout the United States. According to a Head Start worker on the Blackfeet Indian Reservation in Wisconsin, the soaring rates of unemployment, the abject poverty of the people who live there, and the lack of things to do—especially for young people—are key contributors to the problem. "There used to be a show house [movie theater] and a place where they could have dances," he recalls. "We need a burger shop where young people could visit. A lot of their parents drink, so they are not role models. There is also peer pressure."[77]

His observations ring true with his coworkers on the reservation. They know that a steady number of babies born with FAS, who are themselves becoming alcoholic mothers of children with FAS, does not bode well for their future. A health manager for Head Start says that alcoholism is key to every problem for the Blackfeet. It is, she says, "the root of what we struggle with. It's unemployment. It's everything."[78]

A Sioux counselor who creates colorful educational posters for her community says that she is pushing for the prospective fathers to take some initiative. "It's not just women drinking alone—not on the reservation, not anywhere," she says. "It's boyfriends and husbands saying, 'Let's go to a party' or 'Let's have a beer.' If the boyfriends and the husbands would change how they think, it would be much easier for the women to stay clean and sober. It's not their fault alone, but they could help change things."[79]

"She Really Walks the Walk"

There are a number of ways people are being educated about fetal alcohol syndrome. Some of them involve not researchers or doctors but the victims themselves. One sixteen-year-old girl from

Disabled, Not Disobedient

In her article "Tragedy of Fetal Alcohol Damage Is That It's 100 Percent Preventable," former Minnesota first lady Susan Carlson comments on a series of articles by Larry Oakes about Leech Lake Indian Reservation, where FAS is a growing problem. The article appeared in the May 2, 2004, edition of the Star Tribune.

In 1997, while serving as Minnesota's First Lady and also working in juvenile court, I became extremely troubled by what I saw. This is what led to my interest and work in the area of fetal alcohol syndrome (now called [by some] fetal alcohol spectrum disorder, or FASD). Reporter Larry Oakes writes about this disorder affecting most, if not all, of the young people profiled in his series. I find his stories especially tragic because FASD is 100 percent preventable. Unfortunately, our systems are not geared to recognize, identify, or treat this disorder.

Our current approach is to throw resources at these dysfunctional families, hoping to make a difference. In 2000, Hennepin County studied the county's 200 most expensive families and conservatively estimated the cost per family at $145,000 per year. One family had used 29 service providers with little success. The mother and all of her five children suffered from fetal alcohol spectrum disorder. . . .

Research has also shown that identifying those with FASD will reduce secondary effects, including substance abuse and future FASD children, getting into trouble with the law, . . . [and] dropping out of school. . . . FASD is all about brain damage. This diagnosis defines a person as disabled rather than disobedient.

Maine who was born with FAS is traveling around her state with an adoption agency director. Together, they are talking to junior high—and high school—aged teens about FAS.

The girl (unnamed because she is a minor) tells students what her life is like. She explains how even easy homework assignments take "forever," and even though she studies and works very hard, poor grades have kept her off her school's track team.

The agency worker who helps in the presentation has an adopted child with FAS, but students seem to identify more with the girl

In 1999 former president George Bush presents an award to a fetal alcohol syndrome survivor who has dedicated herself to fighting the disorder.

who actually has the disease. "I know about how a parent feels," the worker says, "but she really walks the walk."[80] A teacher who heard the presentation agrees. "You can read about [FAS] in text-books," she says, "but to actually see its effects and be able to discuss it with someone who has experienced the end result has much more of an impact."[81]

Walking Across Ontario

Another FAS sufferer has found another way to educate the public. Tom Wilkinson, a man from Toronto, has undertaken a difficult project. He has decided to walk across the province of Ontario, knock on the door of every brewery, winery, and distillery, and ask them to help fund Canada's first residence for FAS victims.

The project began when his adoptive mother suffered a heart attack. Although she recovered, she said the experience made her worry about Tom, who at twenty-three has the intellect of a seven-year-old. What would happen to him if she had died? "He needs 24-hour supervision," she says, "and that made me think."

She came up with the idea of raising money for a residence by asking the liquor manufacturers themselves to contribute. She wrote letters to all ninety-four such manufacturers in Canada but was disappointed by the response, "I got only twenty replies," she says, "all of them negative except Bacardi-Martini Canada, which gave $1,500. Basically, everybody ignored me."[82]

That angered Tom, who decided to visit the manufacturers personally. In addition to raising money, he says, he hopes that they will include warning labels on liquor bottles, as U.S. manufacturers do. "We want money and we want them to put labels on alcohol like they do on cigarettes," he says. But even if he doesn't raise enough money, Tom says, he believes that he will be able to talk to people along the way and tell them about the disease. "We're not saying we don't want people to drink, just that ladies shouldn't drink when they're pregnant."[83]

High School FAS Experiments

One highly successful program that provided hands-on experience with fetal alcohol syndrome is that of a young Alaska teacher named Stephen Jacquier. He travels from school to school, helping teenagers do laboratory experiments so they can see for themselves the effects of drinking and pregnancy.

The students work with pregnant mice, which have twenty-day gestation periods, or pregnancies. On the ninth day of their gestation, half of the mice are force-fed a small amount of a solution that is 80 percent water and 20 percent grain alcohol. That is equal to a human bingeing on five drinks. Says Jacquier, "It doesn't take much to affect various processes along the way."[84]

The students immediately see the effects of the alcohol on the pregnant mice. The mice stumble around, fall off the edge of a box in their cage, and eventually pass out. However, the more devastating effects are seen ten days later, when the mice are killed and their unborn pups—usually eight or nine per female—are inspected by the students.

The group whose mothers were given the alcohol solution are half the size of the control group, which did not receive alcohol. They also have a range of obvious deformities—a flipper where a paw should be, fused bones, a missing eyeball, even a brain that developed outside the pup's skull. The students keep careful track of what they see, and later compile the data.

The experiments make a powerful impression on the students. Though some say the experience is not enough to make them give up drinking in the future, they all conclude that they never want to be responsible for exposing an unborn child to alcohol. Jacquier believes that the experiments are meaningful because they are done by the students themselves: "They have produced, with their own hands, proof that 'Yes, it's not just all those adults quacking at us.'"[85]

New Discoveries About Alcohol Damage

Many people are involved in educating the public about the dangers of prenatal drinking, and some scientists have made some new discoveries about the way alcohol damages the brain. The scientists have been able to identify the molecules that are responsible for the damage done by alcohol on a developing fetus. "There really haven't been too many clues to start pursuing at the molecular level," says one researcher. "This is the first time a specific molecule has been implicated so clearly."[86]

The molecule, known as L-1, is responsible for guiding the new brain cells to their places in the developing brain. Researchers say that this is accomplished by L-1 allowing the cells to communicate with one another. They can then move to the proper place in the brain and form connections.

To prove the effect of alcohol on the L-1 molecule, scientists gave certain nerve cells growing in laboratory cultures a small amount of alcohol, the equivalent of a human consuming one or two drinks. After being exposed to the alcohol, the cells were unable to find one another, and continued to move around randomly. In a pregnant

Researchers like this biochemist at the University of Arkansas have made important discoveries about the effects of alcohol on the fetus's developing brain.

woman, this would prevent particular parts of the fetus's brain from developing normally.

"You Will Not Reach Your Biological Destiny"

This new research also indicates that alcohol can interfere with another substance that enables cells to communicate called serotonin. Damage to serotonin, explains Dr. John Olney of Washington University, can actually kill the developing cells. When the cells do not receive enough input from other cells, says Olney, "neurons get the message that they are not developing normally. This activates a program that says, 'You will not reach your biological destiny, so kill yourself.'" [87]

In rats, researchers have found that one four-hour bout of alcohol exposure is enough to kill off whole groups of brain cells. Interestingly, by manipulating the time of the exposure—when during the pregnancy the exposure occurs—they can trigger nerve cell death from various regions of the developing fetal brain. For example, a bout of drinking in one stage of pregnancy may harm cells that will help with memory, while in another stage, cells that affect balance or coordination may be affected.

Researchers say that perhaps someday they can develop a chemical that could block the effects of alcohol on serotonin, and on L-1. For now, however, such damage cannot be prevented, and researchers acknowledge that there is no way to know how much alcohol is a risk to the fetus.

Says Dr. James West, a neurobiologist at Texas A&M, "People always ask me, How much is too much? We don't really know. . . . It's unlikely that a drink once in awhile is going to cause any damage, but we don't know for sure." West says that alcohol is so much a part of American culture that people are often unwilling to stop drinking entirely during pregnancy. "If the agent was, say, something in bathroom cleaner," he says, "people would just stay away from it. However, since it is alcohol, and they don't want to give it up, they are interested in how much they can get away with." [88]

"We've Got to Identify These Kids"

While some experts have been working on expanding public awareness or doing scientific research on prenatal alcohol damage, others have been seeking to improve the quality of life for those who already have fetal alcohol syndrome. Some of the most exciting work has been in the diagnosis of FAS, which until now has been sketchy.

Dr. Edward Riley, the chairman of the National Task Force on Fetal Alcohol Syndrome, says that although doctors are able to diagnose newborns with full-blown FAS, they are missing the majority of sufferers, those whose physical symptoms are not as obvious. As a result, tens of thousands of parents and children have not been getting the help they need to understand the disease and its effects. "There may be 80,000 born who do not have the face," he says. "We've got to identify these kids and get them into treatment."[89]

New, more accurate brain scans are showing a great deal of promise for early diagnosis. Scientists reviewing these scans are seeing for the first time that there are several areas of the brain that can be affected by FAS—even in cases where the signature facial abnormalities are absent. These areas of the brain are usually smaller than those of normal children.

The basal ganglia, for example, is a group of nerve cell clusters that help people shift from one activity to another. The damage to this area of the brain may hold the secret of why people with FAS so often have trouble with transitions. The hippocampus, located deep inside the brain, is smaller with FAS, too. This important area is linked to memory.

By doing a scan on a child whose mother is known to have used alcohol during pregnancy, doctors may be able to pinpoint areas of the brain that have been damaged. This would allow special educators to pinpoint those specific weaknesses in their students. "Right now," says one researcher, "these children are treated in any variety of ways that are largely inappropriate [ineffective]."[90]

Facial Screening

One of the problems in identifying the facial abnormalities of the disease is that they sometimes appear in different ways depending on the ethnic background of the victim. The closeness of the eyes, for example, or the flat appearance of the face may be less pronounced in some Native American children, for instance, than

A multi-ethnic group of children with FAS poses for a photo. The facial abnormalities each child exhibits depends largely on their ethnic background.

in children from Russia or Poland. And children whose physical symptoms are less pronounced may not be diagnosed accurately. "Some children exhibit classic features of FAS," says one expert, "and other children have a more mild, less visually obvious version of the disorder, which may not be as recognizable, but still can result in learning disabilities and behavioral disorders."[91]

At the Indiana School of Medicine, scientists are studying the facial characteristics of children with FAS with sophisticated new facial recognition technology. It is based on the same system that is used to identify terrorists who may try to enter U.S. borders at airports. In looking for FAS, scientists hope to establish key points to recognize the disease in any child, regardless of ethnic background.

Each child being screened is photographed from three angles. Using computer software that focuses on key points, such as the space between the eyes, the size of the upper lip, and the distance from ear to ear, researchers create a three-dimensional image, which is then fed into a database. By assembling hundreds of images, scientists hope to make a foolproof standard by which they can compare children suspected of having alcohol effects.

Scientists say that the images can also help identify FAS in young children from all over the world waiting to be adopted. By diagnosing them based on a video, technicians can inform prospective parents about the child's condition and give them information that will help prepare them for raising a child with FAS. Also, the early, accurate diagnosis the scans could provide will help children get the services they need at an early age, when such help will do the most good.

Being Advocates for Those with FAS

Finally, there are new ideas for families of children with FAS that are helping them grow up to achieve their greatest potential. FAS expert Dr. Sterling Clarren at the University of Washington has said that, to one degree or another, those with FAS will always need what he calls an "external brain"—support and guidance—throughout their lives. The external brain may be parents or other family members, counselors, therapists, teachers, or caseworkers.

Because there are so many risks for adolescents and adults with bad decision-making skills, poor impulse control, and/or below-average intelligence, it is hard for a parent alone to help them. Writes one advocate, "My son John's brain does not always function, so he needs my brain to be working for him. And he needs more than one external brain. We have several on-hand: myself, his brother, a mentor volunteer, his job coach, his music group leader. . . . There has to be one available at all times for John to succeed (not get arrested, in trouble, or killed), because his brain may function at any given time at any age level from 4 to 24."[92]

The emphasis on setting up such support systems has helped parents of individuals with FAS come to grips with the notion that no matter how old their children get, their condition will not change. One mother confided that she tended to be more critical and impatient with her daughter when she grew to adulthood. "It's hard to look at a 35-year-old woman and remember that inside she's a little girl," she says. "I have to tell myself that she's only physically bigger, not intellectually or emotionally. It's wrong for me to expect any different."[93]

Not a Random Thing

As more is learned about fetal alcohol syndrome and as it can be diagnosed earlier, things will improve for victims of the disease. They will not be thought of as intentionally bad or slow, or blamed for the inappropriateness of their actions.

"We would never blame a person who is sight impaired if he were to bump into a table and knock over a vase," argues Teresa Kellerman. "We would never blame a person who is hearing impaired if she didn't follow instructions she could not hear. We would never judge a person who could not walk for choosing not to participate in a foot race. Instead, we would advocate for these persons to receive the assistive devices needed for them to participate in life in as normal a capacity as reasonably possible."[94]

Those born with FAS are living with a disability they had no part in creating. And while some victims, with love and support, have carved out a life of their own, many rely on help and supervision. The limits they face are permanent.

"You know, when we first got Benny," says Denise, "we used to think, 'Wow, this is a new beginning. There's no limit to what this little guy might do when he grows up. Maybe president, maybe

Help from the External Brain

In her article "External Brain," Teresa Kellerman, who has an adult son with FAS, describes his need for people to help him make good decisions. In this excerpt, she explains the range of areas in which such a support system is crucial.

Some teens only need an external time-keeper or external change-maker. Others might need an external friend-chooser. Some adults will need an external alarm clock or external budget manager. Many will need a hygiene monitor. Most will need an external decision-maker. Whatever kind of external brain is needed, it should be one that is working properly, that can be vigilant to foresee potential problems to prevent difficult situations in the first place. The external brain definitely needs to be trained in the area of [FAS] issues, and should have a good understanding of the individual's talents and deficits.

The level of support or supervision will depend on the individual's specific abilities and disabilities. A family can determine the level needed for their child by assessing the risk factors in the child's teen years and recent history of events in the person's life. Making a list of situations that have resulted in serious problems or presented high risk for the individual or others can help to demonstrate the level of guidance that is needed. . . . Again, that external brain needs to be in good working order.

Caring parents like these provide the love and support children with fetal alcohol syndrome need to cope with the difficulties of the disease.

a rock star, maybe he'll play for the [Minnesota] Timberwolves, who knows?' We thought about when he got older, what kind of student he'd be in school, his getting married, us having grand-children. It's fun, just thinking about the future.

"But this FAS is a kicker. It's made us aware very early that there will be very rigid limits for Benny. He's not going to have the abilities or skills that other kids have." Denise says that the most important thing people need to understand about FAS is that, unlike most disorders and diseases, FAS is preventable. "It's not a virus, not some weird genetic disease, not some random thing that scientists haven't discovered yet," she says. "It's just pregnant women drinking, and their unborn babies being poisoned. No big mystery. It can't be cured, but it's completely preventable. And that's what makes it so frustrating."[95]

Notes

Introduction: "Where Do I Start?"

1. Denise, interview with author, Inver Grove Heights, MN, May 11, 2004.

Chapter 1: A Devastating Disease

2. Quoted in Michael Dorris, *The Broken Cord: A Family's Ongoing Struggle with Fetal Alcohol Syndrome.* New York: Harper & Row, 1989, p. 144.
3. Quoted in Edith Fairman Cooper, "Alcohol Use and Abuse by Women," Congressional Research Service, September 13, 1991. www.come-over.to/FAS/congress.htm.
4. Quoted in Sheila B. Blume, *What You Can Do to Prevent Fetal Alcohol Syndrome.* Minneapolis: Johnson Institute, 1992, p. 5.
5. Darla, interview with author, Minneapolis, MN, May 21, 2004.
6. Twyla, interview with author, Sioux Falls, SD, June 12, 2004.
7. Twyla, interview.
8. Quoted in *Last Call: The Sobering Truth About FAS/FAE,* VHS. Medford, OR: Advantage Source, 2001.
9. Ida, interview with author, Minneapolis, May 2, 2004.
10. Quoted in Jeff Glasser, "Cycle of Shame," *U.S. News & World Report,* May 20, 2002, p. 26.
11. Mary, telephone interview, May 20, 2004.
12. Lisle, interview with author, Minneapolis, June 3, 2004.
13. Anne, interview with author, Richfield, MN, May 2, 2004.
14. Lynne, telephone interview, May 1, 2004.

Chapter 2: How Alcohol Does Its Damage

15. Quoted in *Last Call.*
16. Dorris, *The Broken Cord,* p. 147.

17. Quoted in *Last Call.*
18. Quoted in *Last Call.*
19. Quoted in *Last Call.*
20. Quoted in Dorris, *The Broken Cord,* p. 154.
21. Terry, telephone interview, April 30, 2004.
22. Quoted in Dorris, *The Broken Cord,* p. 158.
23. Quoted in Elizabeth Rosenthal, "When a Pregnant Woman Drinks," *New York Times,* February 4, 1990, p. SM30.
24. Quoted in Jane Kwiatkowski, "Damage Done," *Buffalo News,* November 12, 2002, p. C1.
25. Sherri, interview with author, Sioux Falls, SD, June 13, 2004.
26. Sherri, interview.
27. Darla, interview.
28. Patty, telephone interview, May 28, 2004.
29. Jean, telephone interview, June 2, 2004.
30. Rob, interview with author, Minneapolis, May 9, 2004.
31. Name withheld, interview with author, June 3, 2004.

Chapter 3: Children with Fetal Alcohol Syndrome
32. Rob, interview with author, May 10, 2004.
33. Name withheld, interview with author, June 2, 2004.
34. Geneva, telephone interview, April 24, 2004.
35. Quoted in Kathleen Longcore, "Delicate Balance," *Grand Rapids Press,* August 14, 2002, p. D3.
36. Name withheld, interview with author, June 1, 2004.
37. Denise, interview.
38. Jean, interview.
39. Rob, interview.
40. Quoted in Judith Kleinfeld and Siobhan Wescott, eds., *Fantastic Antone Succeeds: Experiences in Educating Children with Fetal Alcohol Syndrome.* Fairbanks: University of Alaska Press, 1993, p. 172.
41. Patty, interview.
42. Name withheld, interview with author, May 18, 2004.
43. Quoted in Kleinfeld and Wescott, *Fantastic Antone Succeeds,* p. 134.
44. Quoted in Kleinfeld and Wescott, *Fantastic Antone Succeeds,* p. 159.
45. Quoted in Kleinfeld and Wescott, *Fantastic Antone Succeeds,* p. 106.
46. Name withheld, interview with author, June 2, 2004.

47. Dorris, *The Broken Cord*, p. 111.
48. Dorris, *The Broken Cord*, p. 110.
49. Lynne, interview.
50. Anne, telephone interview, June 8, 2004.
51. Quoted in Judith Kleinfeld and Siobhan Wescott, eds., *Fantastic Antone Grows Up*. Fairbanks: University of Alaska Press, 2000, p. 50.
52. Name withheld, interview with author, May 1, 2004.
53. Earl, interview with author, Minneapolis, May 14–15, 2004.

Chapter 4: Adults with Fetal Alcohol Syndrome
54. Earl, interview.
55. Name withheld, interview with author, June 13, 2004.
56. Rosenthal, "When a Pregnant Woman Drinks."
57. Jean, interview.
58. Name withheld, interview with author, June 3, 2004.
59. Dorris, *The Broken Cord*, p. 251.
60. Dorris, *The Broken Cord*, p. 254.
61. Quoted in Kleinfeld and Wescott, *Fantastic Antone Grows Up*, p. 200.
62. Dorris, *The Broken Cord*, p. 257.
63. Name withheld, interview with author, June 13, 2004.
64. Name withheld, interview with author, May 31, 2004.
65. Quoted in Kleinfeld and Wescott, *Fantastic Antone Grows Up*, p. 236.
66. Name withheld, interview with author, May 31, 2004.
67. Name withheld, interview with author, June 11, 2004.
68. Lilian, interview with author, Sioux Falls, SD, June 11, 2004.
69. Louise, interview with author, Richfield, MN, April 16, 2004.
70. Earl, interview.
71. Bob, telephone interview, April 14, 2004.
72. Quoted in Kleinfeld and Wescott, *Fantastic Antone Grows Up*, p. 4.
73. Earl, interview.

Chapter 5: Making Strides Against FAS
74. Quoted in Kwiatkowski, "Damage Done," p. C1.
75. Quoted in Adam Jackson, "Group Targets Fetal Alcohol Syndrome," *South Bend Tribune*, February 26, 2001, p. 1.

76. *Times-Picayune* (New Orleans), "Drinking for Two," July 19, 2002, p. B6.

77. Quoted in Anita Weier, "Blackfeet Battle Against the Bottle," *Madison Capital Times*, August 17, 2002, p. 5A.

78. Quoted in Weier, "Blackfeet Battle Against the Bottle," p. 5A.

79. Ida, interview.

80. Quoted in Ruth-Ellen Cohen, "Pair Promotes FAS Awareness," *Bangor Daily News*, November 17, 2000, p. 1.

81. Quoted in Cohen, "Pair Promotes FAS Awareness," p. 1.

82. Quoted in Jim Wilkes, "Trek Takes Aim at Alcohol Makers," *Toronto Star*, April 17, 2001, p. B5.

83. Quoted in Wilkes, "Trek Takes Aim at Alcohol Makers," p. B5.

84. Quoted in Dan Joling, "Alaskan Teaches Students How Alcohol, Pregnancy Don't Mix," *Los Angeles Times*, December 10, 2000, p. B4.

85. Quoted in Joling, "Alaskan Teaches Students How Alcohol, Pregnancy Don't Mix," p. B4.

86. Quoted in Ed Edelson, "Research Finds Molecular Cause of Fetal Alcohol Syndrome," *Forbes.com*, June 9, 2003. www.forbes.com/health/feeds/hscout/2003/06/09/hscout513538.html.

87. Quoted in Damaris Christensen, "Sobering Work," *Science News*, July 8, 2000, p. 28.

88. Quoted in Christensen, "Sobering Work," p. 28.

89. Quoted in Hilary Waldman, "Alcohol's Legacy," *Hartford Courant*, October 20, 2002, p. 10.

90. Quoted in Waldman, "Alcohol's Legacy," p. 10.

91. Quoted in *Medical News Today*, "High-Tech Phrenology to Identify Children with Fetal Alcohol Syndrome," April 20, 2004. www.medicalnewstoday.com/newssearch.php?newsid=7425.

92. Teresa Kellerman, "External Brain," FAS Community Resource Center, 2003. www.come-over.to/FAS/externalbrain.htm.

93. Name withheld, interview with author, June 11, 2004.

94. Kellerman, "External Brain."

95. Denise, interview.

Organizations to Contact

FAS Family Resource Institute
PO Box 2525 Lynnwood, WA 98036
(253) 531-2878
www.fetalalcoholsyndrome.org

This nonprofit organization is dedicated to identifying, understanding, and caring for individuals disabled by FAS and their families, and to preventing future generations from being victimized by the disease.

Fetal Alcohol Syndrome Diagnostic and Prevention Network (FASDPN)
University of Washington
PO Box 357920 Seattle, WA 98195-7920
(206) 685-9320
www.depts.washington.edu/fasdpn

The FASDPN is a network of five Washington community clinics whose mission is primary and secondary prevention of FAS through screening, diagnosis, intervention, training, education, and research of this disease. Since 1993, the FASDPN has diagnosed more than fifteen hundred patients, and has provided valuable information to their families.

National Organization on Fetal Alcohol Syndrome (NOFAS)
900 Seventeenth St. NW, Suite 910 Washington, DC 20006
(202) 785-4585
www.nofas.org

Founded in 1990, NOFAS is a nonprofit organization that strives to eliminate the number-one cause of mental retardation by pro viding educational information on its Web site and supporting research on the disease.

For Further Reading

Books

Andrew Barr, *Drink: A Social History of America.* New York: Carroll and Graf, 1999. Good discussion of society's views throughout history concerning pregnant women using alcohol.

FAS/FAE Support Network of British Columbia, *The Art of Making a Difference.* Surrey, BC, 1997. This book is a guide for elementary school teachers and parents, but its information about the learning disabilities of children with FAS is helpful to anyone.

Gary McCuen, *Born Hooked: Poisoned in the Womb.* Hudson, WI: Gem, 1994. Covers the damage to unborn children from alcohol as well as other drugs. Good section on alcohol use on Indian reservations.

Periodicals

Linda Carroll, "Alcohol's Toll on Fetuses: Even Worse than Thought," *New York Times,* November 4, 2003.

Geulah Grossman, "A Small, Delicate Drinking Problem," *Jerusalem Post,* April 5, 2002.

Elizabeth Manning, "Federal Funds to Fight FAS," *Anchorage Daily News,* November 16, 2001.

Howard Pankratz, "Court Says State Can't Jail Mom to Save Fetus," *Denver Post,* May 23, 2003.

Rena Singer, "Apartheid's Unexpected Legacy," *Boston Globe,* September 18, 2001.

Works Consulted

Books

Sheila B. Blume, *What You Can Do to Prevent Fetal Alcohol Syndrome.* Minneapolis: Johnson Institute, 1992. Easy reading, with helpful information on ways women can determine if they may be at risk for having a baby with FAS.

Michael Dorris, *The Broken Cord: A Family's Ongoing Struggle with Fetal Alcohol Syndrome.* New York: Harper & Row, 1989. Considered a classic by experts in FAS, this book provides a frank look at the heartaches in raising a child with FAS.

Judith Kleinfeld and Siobhan Wescott, eds., *Fantastic Antone Grows Up.* Fairbanks: University of Alaska Press, 2000. Helpful information about adolescents and adults with FAS. Good index and bibliography.

———, *Fantastic Antone Succeeds: Experiences in Educating Children with Fetal Alcohol Syndrome.* Fairbanks: University of Alaska Press, 1993. Excellent source with first-person accounts of children with FAS, as well as their parents.

Ann Streissguth, *Fetal Alcohol Syndrome: A Guide for Families and Communities.* Baltimore: Paul H. Brookes, 1997. Very clinical and difficult reading, but excellent background on the causes of the disease.

Periodicals

Belfast News Letter, "Drinking Mothers Damage Unborn Babies," March 21, 2001.

Susan Carlson, "Tragedy of Fetal Alcohol Damage Is That It's 100 Percent Preventable," *Minneapolis Star Tribune,* May 2, 2004.

Ruth-Ellen Cohen, "Pair Promotes FAS Awareness," *Bangor Daily News,* November 17, 2000.

Damaris Christensen, "Sobering Work," *Science News,* July 8, 2000.

Jeff Glasser, "Cycle of Shame," *U.S. News & World Report,* May 20, 2002.

Linda Heinen, "Homeschooling a Child with Fetal Alcohol Syndrome," *Practical Homeschooling,* November/December 2001.

Adam Jackson, "Group Targets Fetal Alcohol Syndrome," *South Bend Tribune,* February 26, 2001.

Dan Joling, "Alaskan Teaches Students How Alcohol, Pregnancy Don't Mix," *Los Angeles Times,* December 10, 2000.

Jane Kwiatkowski, "Challenged at Birth," *Buffalo News,* November 12, 2002.

————, "Damage Done," *Buffalo News,* November 12, 2002.

Kathleen Longcore, "Delicate Balance," *Grand Rapids Press,* August 14, 2002.

Elizabeth Rosenthal, "When a Pregnant Woman Drinks," *New York Times,* February 4, 1990.

Times-Picayune (New Orleans), "Drinking for Two," July 19, 2002.

Hilary Waldman, "Alcohol's Legacy," *Hartford Courant,* October 20, 2002.

Anita Weier, "Blackfeet Battle Against the Bottle," *Madison Capital Times,* August 17, 2002.

Jim Wilkes, "Trek Takes Aim at Alcohol Makers," *Toronto Star,* April 17, 2001.

Internet Sources

Edith Fairman Cooper, "Alcohol Use and Abuse by Women," Congressional Research Service, September 13, 1991. www.come-over.to/FAS/congress.htm.

Ed Edelson, "Research Finds Molecular Cause of Fetal Alcohol Syndrome," *Forbes.com,* June 9, 2003. www.forbes.com/health/feeds/hscout/2003/06/09/hscout513538.html.

Teresa Kellerman, "External Brain," FAS Community Resource Center 2003. www.come-over.to/FAS/externalbrain.htm.

Medical News Today, "High-Tech Phrenology to Identify Children with Fetal Alcohol Syndrome," April 20, 2004. www.medical newstoday.com/newssearch.php?newsid=7425.

Video

Last Call: The Sobering Truth About FAS/FAE. VHS. Medford, OR: Advantage Source, 2001.

Index

Picture Credits

Cover photo: © David Young-Wolff/Photo Edit
AP/Wide World Photos, 23, 30, 38, 43, 46, 49, 55, 72, 80, 83
© Bettmann/CORBIS, 29, 74
© CORBIS, 14
© Bob Daemmrich/Photo Edit, 50
© The Image Bank by Getty Images, 21
Brandy Noon, 18, 33, 35
© Bob Rowen; Progressive Image/CORBIS, 64, 68
© David H. Wells/CORBIS, 11, 90
© David Young-Wolff/Photo Edit, 41, 59, 62, 67, 77, 86

About the Author

Gail B. Stewart received her undergraduate degree from Gustavus Adolphus College in St. Peter, Minnesota. She did her graduate work in English, linguistics, and curriculum study at the College of St. Thomas and the University of Minnesota. She taught English and reading for more than ten years.

She has written over ninety books for young people, including a series for Lucent Books called The Other America. She has written many books on historical topics such as World War I and the Warsaw ghetto.

Stewart and her husband live in Minneapolis with their three sons, Ted, Elliot, and Flynn; two dogs; and a cat. When she is not writing, she enjoys reading, walking, and watching her sons play soccer.